SUCCESSFUL COLD CALL SELLING

Second Edition

SUCCESSFUL COLD CALL SELLING

Second Edition

Lee Boyan

amacom

American Management Association

This book is available at a special
discount when ordered in bulk quantities.
For information, contact Special Sales Department,
AMACOM, a division of American Management Association,
135 West 50th Street, New York, NY 10020.

Library of Congress Cataloging-in-Publication Data

Boyan, Lee.
    Successful cold call selling.

    Includes index.
    1. Selling.   2. Direct selling.
3. Telephone selling.   I. Title.
HF5438.25.B68   1989   658.8'5   88-48041
ISBN 0-8144-7718-6

Printing number

10 9 8 7 6 5 4 3 2 1

WHAT THIS BOOK WILL DO FOR YOU

You are about to learn powerful, proven techniques that will enable you to perform at your best whenever you introduce yourself to a new prospect either in person or by phone. You will master the ability to gain an audience that has top-level buying authority as you arrange to present your offering under the most favorable circumstances, and you will come out with orders where no business previously existed.

To be able to do this self-assuredly and consistently is heady wine indeed. There is and always will be insatiable demand for persons with such skill.

My thirty-five years of experience as a salesperson, field sales trainer, seminar leader, professional speaker, and management consultant have provided me with countless opportunities to meet thousands of sales executives from all kinds of businesses. My association with them was often more than a casual acquaintance. Many times we worked closely together, planning sales campaigns, sales meetings, and training programs, and developing new concepts to use in my sales and management seminars.

I have learned a great deal from my association with these executives. If I had to single out the one skill they value most of all in their men and women, it would be the ability to create new business instead of just being order takers.

Taking orders for something buyers are ready and waiting to buy at a price they are willing to pay can usually be done by salespeople with average ability. But the highest rewards, both financial and intangible, go to those who are able to create new business through their ingenious efforts.

Do you ever feel uneasy when you make an introductory call to a new prospect either by phone or in person?

Do you prefer to call on repeat customers or familiar prospects rather than strangers?

Do you feel that making "cold calls" is unproductive?

Do you ever get thrown off balance by a harsh rebuff?

When an appointment is canceled or a call is finished sooner than expected, do you often find yourself without fill-in prospects to call on?

Do you often have difficulty getting past a receptionist or a secretary?

Do you often have to settle for making presentations to persons who do not have buying authority?

Do you ever find yourself at a loss for words when a prospect resists granting you an interview?

Do you ever wish you could have a second chance to make a particular first impression?

Do you often find it difficult to gain the attention of prospects who are preoccupied with other important matters?

Do you have an effective strategy for dealing with these situations?

If you answered yes to any question except the last one, you will find specific ideas in *Successful Cold Call Selling* that will vastly increase your selling power.

If you answered no to the last question, this book will help you build a selling strategy that will change your selling career for the better, once and for all.

I have seen dramatic positive changes in the performance of many salespeople, some who doubled and tripled their sales production after learning just a few of the techniques set forth in this book. In some cases they were shy even to the point of being called introverted. Yet today they are enjoying high incomes plus newly found self-confidence by creatively selling big-ticket products and services to top-level executives.

When you master the techniques revealed in this book, you too will gain a great deal of personal and economic security. You will never be out of a job. You can, on your own initiative, increase your income any time you want. You will also have a most rewarding feeling of poise and a sense of control over the direction of your life—poise not only in the business world of selling, but also in the entire range of interpersonal relationships.

If you practice the counselor style of selling, you will find much in this book to ensure that you are conducting your counselor interview effectively with key decision makers. And the techniques described here will help you to avoid wasting your time and energy with those who merely serve as gatekeepers.

In addition to many new interpretations and greater expansion of the original content, this second edition contains 116 new ideas, scripts, examples, and insights. For example, you learn how to make cold calls when you must interface with sophisticated, high-tech answering devices such as voice mail.

In this second edition of *Successful Cold Call Selling,* you will learn how to:

- Identify causes of fear
- Control your emotions
- Conquer the fear of making cold calls
- Gain self-confidence
- Eliminate call reluctance
- Get in the right frame of mind to make cold calls

- Decide what you want to happen and make it happen
- Design a strategy for getting new business
- Plan your opening move
- Decide on the method of approach
- Create effective opening statements that open doors
- Put the right words together
- Avoid commonly used, ineffective words and phrases
- Find prospects from a variety of often overlooked sources
- Get and use referrals
- Determine who makes the decision
- Avoid getting trapped with the wrong person
- Deal with lower-level authority
- Dialog with receptionists and secretaries
- Create an irresistible invitation to hear your presentation
- Approach large organizations
- Get appointments with high-level executives
- Come across with confidence and authority
- Get through to the unreachable prospect
- Keep on course toward your objective
- Set up the ideal selling situation
- Use the magic door opener
- Position yourself in the prospect's mind
- Eliminate a prospect's defensiveness
- Relax the tough prospect
- Qualify prospects
- Avoid negative prejudgment
- Get on the prospect's wavelength
- Quickly build rapport
- Open a closed mind
- Disarm hostility
- Create a climate of trust
- Ask the right questions for a successful initial contact
- Use a dramatic tool often overlooked in communication
- Turn a negative situation into a positive one
- Use precall letters
- Conduct a needs analysis
- Isolate the main issue
- Uncover hidden needs

- Deal with indifference, skepticism, procrastination, complacency, repetitive objections, disgruntled former customers, and "just send a brochure"
- Avoid copouts
- Keep yourself relaxed
- Avoid broken appointments
- Deal with prospects under pressure
- Keep the odds in your favor
- Ask "why" tactfully
- Close for appointments
- Secure the best presentation setting
- Get business away from the competition
- Sharpen your telephone skills
- Avoid sounding canned
- Be effectively persistent without being pushy
- Set up callbacks
- Cope with your own frustrations and tensions
- Enjoy the rich rewards of being a sales professional
- Take it all to the bank

If you are a

new salesperson, this book will help you to quickly gain self-confidence and get you off to a fast start.

seasoned veteran, you will sharpen your skills and become motivated to go after new accounts.

sales manager or a sales trainer, you will get many ideas to help you train and motivate your salespeople to get new accounts.

small business owner, you will ensure continuing sales and profits.

It is important to read and understand each chapter in proper sequence. In later chapters you will be given specific techniques and explicit words and phrases to use at the point of introduction to a new prospect that are sure to open new doors for you. But the words and phrases will ring true and the techniques will work their magic only if you fully understand and adhere to the principles that unfold in the earlier chapters. Although some of these principles extend to all phases of selling, this book concerns primarily their all-important impact during the opening move.

Now let's begin your first step on the way to building your strategy for successful cold call selling.

Lee Boyan

CONTENTS

Chapter 1

HOW COLD IS A COLD CALL?

The question I get asked most often from members of my seminar audiences is, "Lee, what did you ever sell?"

Fair question. Let me answer it here as well—I assume the readers of this book are much like members of my training sessions.

Very early on, I sold cookware direct to the consumer. That's not the easiest thing to sell, but it is a good place to learn. You learn fast. Because if you don't learn, you don't eat when you are paid straight commission only.

I sold quite a bit the first month. I sold my boat, my second car, my skis.

Then I sold radio advertising. That is one of the most intangible things you can sell. If advertisers don't listen to the spots, all the clients get is an invoice at the end of the month. My job at the station was developing new business. So I made a lot of cold calls.

For the last twenty-five years, I've been selling, and still do sell, sales training programs and consulting services. When I

1

make a cold call on a top-level executive and say, "Mr. or Ms. Executive, my special reason for calling on you today is to show you an idea that my clients tell me helps their salespeople to generate more new business," I'm on the spot. Because I am expected to demonstrate personally that I practice what I preach when I make my presentation.

I'm not telling you this to toot my horn, but rather, so you will know I'm not an armchair professor. We are going to concern ourselves with proven principles and techniques that have been tested in the real world.

I get some interesting reactions to the title of this book and my seminars. People say, "We don't make cold calls. We get inquiries from advertising." Or, "We get leads from trade shows." Or, "We work by referral."

Even if you use these methods, at some point you must make an initial contact with a prospect either by phone or in person. That is what this book is all about: how to make that initial contact effectively.

Then some say, "We don't make cold calls because we get repeat business from regular customers." A common error salespeople make when calling on regular customers is the failure to begin the interview properly. It is, of course, unspoken, but too often their manner seems to say, "Well, here I am again." Then they let the customer set the tone and direction. But every call, in a sense, *is* a cold call. Customers are usually preoccupied at the moment you approach. You must help them make the transition from what they are thinking about to what you want them to think about. Salespeople calling on regular customers would make more effective calls if they got rid of the notion that they don't make cold calls and put into practice methods and techniques of successful cold call selling.

Even those who do get business from regular customers need to get some new accounts from time to time. There is generally a 20 percent turnover of accounts because of changes in the marketplace. And that figure is increasing in this age of downsizing, mergers, early retirement, and frequent job changes. That dependable, friendly, familiar customer you had for years may no longer be there. You may have to start from scratch with a *cold call on a new buyer at an old account!*

We think of competition as others in our industry selling similar products or services. But competition for prospects' time is an equally important consideration. Suppose you have a high-priority target prospect you are trying to reach. For the past several weeks he has been besieged by a parade of sales reps selling a wide variety of products and services. Here you come along on the tail end of the parade. You are likely to be odd person out.

Look what is happening in the marketplace. As we change from a smokestack to an information economy, more new products and services are being sold. Consider what the micro chip has done to our world. Since banks became deregulated, they and savings and loan associations are hiring salespeople to sell their new products and services. Now that Ma Bell has split up, the telephone business is proliferating. I often have attorneys and certified public accountants in my seminars: They need to go after new business too. The point is, more salespeople are pounding the pavement and punching telephone buttons than ever before. You are competing with all these salespeople for the time and attention of the same prospects you call on, no matter what product or service others sell.

Perhaps it's the term itself that is part of the problem that makes this type of call difficult for too many salespeople. One dictionary lists these synonyms for the word *cold:* inhospitable, unsociable, unwelcome, forbidding, unfriendly, ungracious, uncordial, unapproachable. I can just see someone identifying with those definitions and adding, perhaps subconsciously, this one—unworthy of my time and risk to my sensitive ego.

A Roadblock to Be Removed

The problem is not just that most salespeople prefer business to come in the easy way. The commonplace yet subtle reality is—fear. Fear of possible rejection in that seemingly inhospitable, unsociable, unwelcome, forbidding, unfriendly territory. Fear of appearing awkward and feeling embarrassed in an unpredictable personal encounter.

In my experience working with salespeople in the field, I've met countless who have all the tools to become outstanding. They have the intelligence, looks, pleasing personality, and product knowledge, but they don't put those gifts to full use because of fear of the threat to their ego. They prefer to call on a familiar friendly customer who may not offer the sales potential of prospects more difficult to get in to see. They spend more time than necessary in the office setting up calls, shuffling through prospect cards, or in the car traveling from one call to another—and passing all kinds of good prospects along the way. It is easier to sit comfortably behind the wheel, listening to the stereo, watching the scenery go by, than it is to be face to face with a prospect and risk rejection. It is easier to justify any kind of work activity, even if it's not productive. I've often heard, "Gee, I left the house at seven o'clock in the morning, didn't get back until nine o'clock at night." But most of the time was spent driving. The only people who get paid for driving automobiles are chauffeurs and cab drivers and they usually don't get paid very much. Of course, there is necessary distance to travel between calls and the urgency of a prospect ready to buy may determine the travel distance. But the issue here is to be honest with ourselves—are we avoiding a perceived risk of rejection, are we hanging on to the roof instead of playing our tune?

Before we consider the techniques of making cold calls, we must give some thought to neutralizing the negative effect of fear. For if there is fear, there is likely to be call reluctance. And if there is call reluctance, any discussion of techniques is strictly academic.

Chapter 2

TRIUMPH OVER FEAR

Rarely do sales training programs deal with the subject of fear. From my discussions with sales executives, I find that the reason it is avoided is that it is considered to be negative. I don't buy that. Positive thinking doesn't mean that you close your eyes to reality. Much has been said about how easy it is to sell, how quickly money can be made—"All you gotta do is act enthusiastic." All of which often doesn't connect with what is going on in the solar plexus of the salesperson standing before an indifferent, preoccupied, sometimes unfriendly prospect. I believe it is a positive approach to train salespeople how to accept the reality of fear and how to deal with it.

Admitting Fear

The starting point for building skill in making uninvited initial contacts with prospective buyers is to recognize, admit, and then control the normal fear of disapproval and rejection.

5

To deny it is to set in motion all sorts of immobilizing defense mechanisms. When your conscious mind denies a feeling, it goes underground and continues to affect your feelings in unconscious ways over which you have little or no control.

Most salespeople experience fear. It's nothing to be ashamed of. So be honest. Bring fear out into the open. Then go to work to deal with it. There is no legitimate reason for anyone to deny the normal emotions all salespeople feel at one time or another. Admit you don't like to call on people who don't want to see you. And you don't relish talking about something you feel they don't want to talk about. That's natural. We all have an ebb and flow to our feelings and to our ambition.

The Causes of Fear

Once we identify the causes of fear, we can concentrate on removing the causes and the fears will begin to fade away. Here are the most common causes of fear of making cold calls:

- Lack of skill
- Need for approval
- Faulty perception of reality
- Poor self-image
- Negative self-talk

Lack of Skill

When you lack skill, you lack confidence. When you lack confidence, you will experience fear.

What is it you need to learn that would make you more competent, therefore more confident, on your job? What do you need to learn about the product or service you sell, or about its application to your customer's needs? What do you need to learn about selling skills?

Write these items down. Then set goals to learn them. It

doesn't do much good to identify your needs unless you make a commitment to do something about them.

An effective marketing concept is known as *positioning*. The idea here is for a company to position itself as the number one supplier of the product or service it sells in the minds of the customers and prospective customers in its market niche. A good way to understand the positioning concept is to answer this question; Who was the second person to fly the Atlantic? It's a safe bet you don't know. But you certainly know who was the first.

Likewise, strive to become the number one supplier of what you sell in the minds of the customers and prospective customers in your market niche. In other words, become so knowledgeable about what you sell that your customers will want to do business with you exclusively. They will because you understand their needs and problems and are better able to address and satisfy those needs than any of your competitors. This is a positioning over and above any positioning your company may have done. *You are added value*. Granted this doesn't happen overnight, but this is the status to which you aspire. When you reach it, your confidence will be so invincible that you will have no difficulty making cold calls.

Birth of a Salesperson

Fred Hawkins sells industrial supplies for a distributing firm that maintains an inventory from many different manufacturers. By whatever yardstick you may choose to use, Fred is successful. His income from commissions and bonuses is higher than the income of many of the top-level executives of manufacturers he represents. He thoroughly enjoys his work. Rarely does a month go by without Fred getting recognition for sales achievement in some manufacturer's bulletin. Fred and his wife love to talk about the expense-paid trips he has won to scores of the most fabulous resort spas of the world.

*Names used as examples in this book (for instance, Fred Hawkins) are fictitious.

Whenever Fred makes a sales call, the red carpet is rolled out to greet him. Here is what a plant manager of one of Fred's accounts has to say about him:

> I've asked Fred to call me first whenever he plans to come to my plant. Either I personally take him around to the people he should see or I make appointments for him with department heads, process engineers, or whoever may be involved in a purchasing decision. Fred is a walking reference manual regarding many of the tools and supplies we use. Not just what's what but how best to use them. I have a shop coat for him hanging in my office closet. He wears it nearly every time he's here shoulder to shoulder with people on the shop floor. It's like having a specialist on my staff but he doesn't cost me a cent in payroll or fringe benefits except that I've instructed my people to never let Fred pick up a lunch check.

Fred is the exact opposite of the stereotypical, extroverted, dynamic persuader. Rather, he is a quiet, low-key kind of person. Fred told me:

> I'll never forget those first few weeks when I started selling years ago. Talk about panic city. One call in particular, my hands were shaking so much I couldn't get the briefcase opened. Embarrassing! I was absolutely mortified. My mind must have gone blank because I don't even remember how I got out of there. Next thing I recall was driving up to my next appointment in a cold sweat. This call was on a fairly small manufacturing plant. When I got there I just sat behind the wheel of my car feeling sorry for myself, wishing I had a nice comfortable job where I could work all by myself.
>
> As luck had it, my negative train of thought was distracted when I noticed a truck being loaded at the rear door of the plant. The truck belonged to a machine shop a few blocks away that was also on my prospect list, but was not buying from us. What struck me as odd was that the pieces being loaded on the truck were unfinished components. I guessed these parts were being sent out to the job shop for machining operations this plant couldn't handle. The truck driver confirmed my suspicions. He further told me exactly what the

machining operations were, how many trips he made back and forth each week, and how many pieces were loaded each trip.

Whatever self-pity or fear I had been experiencing quickly evaporated. I recalled that one of our suppliers had just sent us a brochure on a new attachment to a standard machine tool that would be able to handle this job. I suddenly saw my role in a different light. That company really needed me. I had an idea that was going to save them a lot of money. They were going to be glad I chose to call on them that day and that I chanced to park my car where I could see that truck being loaded. I wasn't just another salesman interrupting someone busy with other matters. I had something to show them that was so important, they had just better drop what they were doing and hear me out! I practically ran to the reception desk. I don't even remember what I said to the receptionist but it must have been pretty good because I recall the urgency with which she tracked down Mr. Schaefer, president of the company. When I sat down in his office this time, any fumbling with the briefcase was due to sheer excitement, not fear.

Yes, Mr. Schaefer bought my idea. Although he never was a big account in terms of volume, his business grew over the years and I don't believe he ever bought a product that we carry from any other source.

The most important sale I made that day was to myself when I sold myself on what my job is all about. From that time on I realized there must be hundreds of places in my territory that could improve their procedures in some way, who were using obsolete equipment and inefficient methods that were costing them time, dollars, waste, customer satisfaction, frustration, you name it. And my job was to look for those situations and show them a better way. I didn't see myself as someone selling products, I'm more like a consultant. The products got sold as a result of showing a better way.

Fred Hawkins has never lost his excitement for what he is doing and he doesn't have to put on a phony act to show it, for it is genuine. His enthusiasm is such a sincere and honest emotion that it elicits trust and an equally sincere and honest consideration of his recommendations. It isn't something that Fred just turns on when he is in contact with customers.

Fred is a consummate student of the business. He reads everything he can get his hands on pertaining to the use of his products. He has antennas out, constantly scanning the world he travels in for new ideas and innovations. His world is beyond the office of purchasing agents where his competitors struggle with trying to "overcome objections," unaware of the real reason they are not getting any business. His world is out among the people who are using his products, where buying decisions are actually made. He wants to see what is going on, and he constantly asks questions, to learn ways to be more effective. It's not that he snubs purchasing agents. He actually makes their job easier. He goes where he goes because his customers want him to be there.

Fred rarely has to ask for referrals. Names of prospects are given to him freely. Most often a customer will personally call the prospect and enthusiastically pave the way for him. When Fred does make an unsolicited call, he doesn't have to use any techniques. He just does what comes naturally. The excitement, the urgency, and the credibility surge forth from his reservoir of knowledge and experience.

Fred Hawkins has positioned himself as the number one supplier of what he sells to his market niche.

Need for Approval

The need to gain approval is buried deep in the human psyche. We are conditioned by this need from infancy. As helpless children we really needed acceptance from our parents. Later the need for acceptance became the need for approval—when we learned there was a reward (approval) when we behaved as our parents wanted us to behave and punishment (disapproval) when we didn't. Later still, we conformed to values and behavior of our peers. Not to be approved by them was to suffer feelings of rejection that our tender, young ego could hardly bear. In school much of what we learned was motivated by seeking approval of the teachers and authority figures. On our first job it soon became clear to us that the way to get along, to keep the job, to get a raise in pay, and to get promoted was to gain approval of our boss. The dating and mating game revolves totally around approval not only of our dates and mates but also of their friends and relatives, especially our future in-laws. This is not to speak disparagingly of parents, teachers, bosses, and in-laws. I've served my time as the approver in enough of those roles. That is just the way it is. It's part of the human condition in our society.

But this urge for approval does affect our feelings and resulting performance on our job in the sales profession. It shows up especially when we have to risk taking the initiative to announce our presence and state our business to a prospect who is a stranger and who is preoccupied with other important matters. Rare indeed is the individual who takes that risk calmly, naturally, without proper conditioning or training to counteract the ingrained effect of a lifelong pursuit of approval. It is the purpose of this book to provide you with a course of action that will give you that kind of conditioning and training.

Here are some questions to consider:

- How do I feel when a prospect isn't friendly?
- Is it reasonable to expect instant approval from every prospect?
- Do I need to change my expectations regarding approval?

By answering those questions we may come to realize that some of the problems we have with making cold calls are self-imposed by an unreasonable choice of expectations.

The Mental Dynamics of Expectations

Let's see how the choice of expectations can affect the performance of a salesperson making an unsolicited call on a stranger. Let's call her Harriet.

Harriet represents a printing firm that specializes in high-quality color reproduction for large-volume clients. Harriet is about to make a call on a mail-order merchandiser that has been having catalogs and brochures printed by a competitor.

On the way to her destination, Harriet is thinking, "I sure hate making these cold calls. Maybe I'd better stop for a cup of coffee and figure out how to handle this situation."

She recalled that a salesperson who previously called on Mr. Bullman, the advertising manager of the mail-order house, said he was a hard-nosed character. Harriet's stomach begins to churn! She envisions a gruff-looking individual impatiently meeting her in the reception lobby. She imagines the embarrassment she suffers as Mr. Bullman makes quick work of rejecting her out loud in front of other waiting salespeople.

Harriet wishes she were about to call on a friendly, familiar customer and begins to wonder if it might be better to do just that instead. But her manager has been after her to get some new accounts. In fact, a quarterly performance review is coming up soon and she will have to make an accounting of herself. That could be more painful than facing Mr. Bullman.

Her stomach churns some more! Then she recalls reading somewhere that people always respond to us the way we expect them to respond to us. So expect a positive reception.

"Well," she muses, "that doesn't always work. Matter of fact, the last few cold calls did not turn out to be very positive. There must be something wrong with me. I don't seem to be able to positive-ize my expectations."

Now Harriet is back to square one with the churnings in the pit of her stomach. So she grits her teeth and goes out to make the call despite the fear of being hurt and humiliated. She's like the comic strip character, good ole Charlie Brown, who is up to bat in the bottom of the ninth with two outs and his team behind 60 to 0. But this is not the kind of emotional state for Harriet to be in to perform at her best.

How could Harriet have changed her interpretation of this scenario?

To begin with, Harriet didn't know what kind of reception she was actually going to get from Mr. Bullman. It could be warm and friendly. It could be indifferent. It could be hostile.

So her first mistake was to make an assumption that was extreme. In this case it was extreme—negative. That assumption was biased with someone else's opinion. Opinions are not usually a good source of objective reality.

Harriet was right not to take the other extreme, that is, to expect a positive reception. But of course, she knows better. She's been burned with that one before.

Effective Prejudgment

It would make most sense for Harriet to choose to expect a neutral reception—neither especially warm nor especially cool. The law of averages dictates that that is most likely the way it will actually be. Of course, she would *prefer* the prospect to be agreeable. But if not it's no big deal.

We allow ourselves to become upset when people don't behave the way we want them to. To make matters more upsetting, according to a prevalent false notion in traditional sales lore, we should be able to manipulate people into behaving the way we want. When that doesn't happen we feel inadequate. Brooding over this negative self-judgment further inhibits our ability to perform. It can even immobilize us.

On any given call, chances that you will meet with a difficult prospect are very slight. Even if you do, whatever happens will not ruin your sales career.

It's a fact of life, especially in selling, that people often don't act the way we want them to act. How do we perceive this—as a threat or an opportunity? That is the choice we make. Do we make that choice consciously and deliberately? Or do we allow ourselves to be controlled by negative habit patterns?

The Secret of Security From an Old Pro

I will never forget Ben Moore. Ben was the manager on my very first sales job selling cookware direct to the consumer. It's not the easiest product in the world to sell but it's good for learning how to sell. After a couple of weeks, I hadn't sold a thing. A lot of doors were slammed in my face. Dogs chased me down the street. I had blisters on my hands from carrying those big, heavy sample cases.

One day at lunch I ordered tea and toast.

"You're a pretty skinny guy to be on that kind of diet," the waitress remarked.

"I'm not on a diet. But I'll tell you what I am on. I'm on commission. That's what I'm on."

I went to Ben with my crying towel out. "Ben, I'm just not cut out for this commission selling. There's no security in it."

That struck a nerve. Ben came back to me with, "Security? What are you talking about? Security is how you can do this here job—how you can sell this here cookware. Security is in yourself, boy. Ain't no other place. Security is how you can get in those doors being slammed at ya. Security is how ya gets people to sit down and listen to ya when they're too busy. You'll get yourself a whole bunch of security when ya gets people interested in this cookware after they tells ya they're not interested. Not get out there on the street with those sample cases and don't come cryin' to me about where there ain't no security."

Yes, security must come from within. Security is the knowledge that you can deal with the resistance you encounter. For resistance is the reason for the existence of the sales profession. It's the reason you get paid. And the more skillful you are at dealing with it, the more you will get paid.

To start out the day hoping not to run into any resistance, to look for prospective buyers who always greet you with open arms, is not being realistic. It's true you will meet agreeable buyers once in a while. But if they become too commonplace, you might be out of a job. Your company could get all the distribution it wants without the expense of a sales force. So fortunately for the sales profession, buyers aren't always that easy. Sometimes they will not be especially eager to see you at the particular time you happen to call, even though they could eventually become very interested and could profit from your offering.

One positive expectation you can have: Resistant prospects can provide your best opportunities!

Faulty Perception of Reality

Do you perceive normal indifference as rejection?

Indifference is normal. It is a common response you get from a preoccupied stranger. Are you translating this normal indifference that comes with the territory into something it is not? It is not personal rejection of you. Prospects may reject the notion of spending some time with you at any particular moment, but they are not rejecting you as a person.

Do you make allowances for unknown circumstances that may affect a prospect's mood?

Your prospect may be having a bad day. Perhaps a key employee has just resigned, or a customer has canceled an order. There could be a difficult personal problem, a recent experience with an inept or dishonest salesperson. It could be that the prospect is by nature suspicious or surly. Any number of things could be going on in the prospect's world, of which you are totally unaware, to cause him to be a little testy. Are you responding to an unpleasant mood that may have nothing to do with you?

Do you give prospects credit for more prestige or status than they are due? Are you putting prospects on pedestals they do not deserve?

Your business is just as legitimate as the businesses of the people you call on. Your time is just as valuable as their time. You are equals. They are no more important than you regardless of their title, age, sex, color, race, or position.

As you make your calls, you have an exceptional opportunity to gather all the up-to-date information on the state of the art and trends in your industry. You are like a reporter who observes other people in action. You see different ones using your products and similar products in ways that bring them greater or lesser advantage. You see what works and what doesn't work. You are in a unique position to render valuable, practical expertise. Business firms, institutions, and government units willingly pay high fees to professional consultants for the kind of counsel you can offer free of charge. It is important to incorporate this dimension into the way you see yourself on your job. This bring us to the next cause of fear.

Poor Self-Image

- Do you see yourself as an expert in your field?
- Do you see yourself as a bearer of good news?
- Do you see yourself as a problem solver?

There is a question in the mind of every prospect you approach either on the phone or in person. The question is, "Is this approaching salesperson a pestering time waster or does this person have valuable information I ought to hear about?" You must have an answer to that question. And a good answer to it begins in your own mind—how you see yourself.

Self-image is like a thermostat. You can move the lever on a thermostat to any position you select and the temperature of a room will rise or fall in relation to the set position. It's as if we have a lever in our head that controls our self-image, and we control the lever. We can choose to see ourselves any way we want. Our level of performance will rise or fall according to how we choose to see ourselves. It has been proved in training circles that you cannot teach people to do anything that conflicts with their self-image. In other words, you can perform in your role only in a manner consistent with how you see yourself.

In Chapter 11 I suggest words, phrases, and techniques for getting through to high-level decision makers. You can learn the words, even practice techniques by role-playing with other salespeople in a training session. But the words, phrases, and techniques won't work for you in the real world with a live prospect unless you believe you have every right to an audience with a high-level person. Because if you don't believe you do, you will subconsciously do whatever you have to do to get where you believe you belong.

Please pay special heed to what I personally believe is the single most important piece of advice I can give you about cold call selling. The door-opening words, phrases, and techniques will be effective only to the degree that you understand and put into practice this concept:

IT IS IMPERATIVE THAT YOU SEE YOURSELF AS A COMPETENT, KNOWLEDGEABLE EXPERT IN YOUR FIELD AND THAT YOU HAVE INFORMATION AND IDEAS THAT WILL BE OF BENEFIT TO THE PEOPLE YOU CALL ON. NOT ONLY THE PRODUCT OR SERVICE YOU SELL, BUT *YOU PERSONALLY, BY YOUR INTERCHANGE, WILL BENEFIT THEM.*

If you are new to the job, you can consider yourself a pipeline through which the information flows from the resources in your company to your clientele. Then you must place a high priority on becoming a competent, knowledgeable expert as quickly as you can.

Salespeople often call themselves peddlers. Of course, the term is typically used flippantly or in jest. But I believe there is something deep inside of us that doesn't realize it is being used in jest. Then our validity, our credibility, is tilted away from that delicate balance that often hangs in a prospect's mind as the decision is being made on whether or not to grant an interview.

And when we see ourselves as peddlers, we will become peddlers and time wasters in the prospect's mind because we will look like peddlers and sound like peddlers. Remember what was said earlier about positioning. *Positioning must first happen in our own mind before it can happen in the mind of the prospect.* A strong, positive self-image is the catalyst that makes techniques work. Words and techniques are not nearly as important as the sound of confidence in your voice that asserts you have important information and you know what you are talking about.

Negative Self-Talk

"Cold calls are tough to make."
"I hate making cold calls."

"My prospects don't like salespeople making cold calls."
"Cold calls are unproductive."

Do you say these things to yourself? And what good does that do? It does no good. But it surely does a lot of harm.

Psychologist Albert Ellis, who has written many books on psychology in language for the lay person, expressed the concept this way: "One has enormous control over one's emotions if one chooses to work at controlling them and to practice saying the right kind of sentences to oneself."[1] And Dr. Maxwell Maltz added this in his popular book *Psycho-Cybernetics:* "Ideas are changed, not by 'will,' but by other ideas."[2]

Harnessing the Power to Change

We have the power to replace faulty ideas and wrong assumptions with more constructive ideas when we are aware of this power. Most intelligent people will agree with the axiom that positive thoughts bring positive results and negative thoughts bring negative results. That is, they agree with the concept when they are reading a book or sitting in a seminar on the subject, but that awareness quickly evaporates and often it is not there in the routine, workaday world.

But people who habitually choose negative statements in their inner dialog and in their communication with others seldom realize the damaging power negative choices have upon their lives.

Often in my consulting practice I hear people explain away poor performance with a seemingly logical excuse. They will say, "Our business is different." Then they'll describe problems unique to their business over which they have no control. Yet there are others in the same kind of business with the same set of problems who are doing great! No matter how logical, excuses never have anything to do with the solution to a problem. The solution to a problem must begin with constructive words in the mind and on the lips of the would-be problem solver.

A Failure Turned Into Success

Anna Mae Randall sells an air freight service to customers in Fort Worth. Her customers regularly ship small but valuable cargo from Texas all over the world. One day early in the week she called on a new prospect and persuaded the traffic manager to use her company's service for shipping oil well drilling equipment spare parts frequently needed by drillers in Saudi Arabia, Mexico, the North Sea, and other distant locations. It showed promise of being an excellent account and Anna Mae felt so sure of it that she started phoning other prospects to set up a series of calls for the rest of the week. On Friday she didn't bother to go to her office but went straight to work making her calls. As a result, she didn't learn that the drilling company equipment manager had called to cancel his agreement.

Not knowing about the defunct order, Anna Mae continued working with high expectations. She had the assurance of a successful salesperson and got several more orders. When the day was over she drove home, still without checking in at the office. She later said:

It was the best weekend in years. My husband and I went out on the town to celebrate. I called my boss, who congratulated me on my best week ever. It wasn't until Monday morning that he and I learned that the oil well equipment order had been canceled. I discovered that the success which turned me on for the rest of the week was a failure. By then it didn't matter because the others were so much better. Funny, it was that first order I thought I had and really didn't, that made me get out and hustle to sell still more. Yet, I recall another time I'll have to admit, when a canceled order made me feel so bad, I went into a slump that lasted several weeks.

When Anna Mae told me that, I could only think how important our reactions are and how unimportant our individual failures are when we just do the work we should be doing. When her perceptions were that she was successful, she became successful. When she perceived failure, she made it happen.

How to Control Emotions

It is important to understand that we, like Anna Mae, choose our own response to what is happening to us. Choosing a response begins with an interpretation. That is, we use words to explain what we perceive is going on. We do this verbalizing mentally as self-talk or as we explain it to others. Now we are at the heart of where critical choices are made. We choose the words in our interpretation. The words trigger our feelings and actions, which in turn determine what happens to us.

Computer people have an interesting term known as GIGO, which means garbage in, garbage out. If you put wrong information into a computer, you can't possibly get the right information out. Our subconscious works the same way. It could care less what you feed it. It will act upon what it is fed and bring it up on the CRT screen of your life! Garbage in, garbage out. Success in, success out.

When you say, "Cold calls are tough to make"—they will be. If you say, "I hate making cold calls," you surely will. "Cold calls are unproductive" leads to exactly that. "My prospects don't like salespeople making cold calls." Of course they won't, because you will approach them timidly, tentatively, hesitatingly, when you need to convey the opposite. You need to emanate self-confidence.

We are saying both positive and negative sentences to ourselves most of our waking hours, whether we are aware of it or not. A good way to practice saying the right kind of sentences, Dr. Ellis recommends, is to make a habit of repeating selected positive affirmations several times every day. Here is an example:

I am a confident, competent professional with special knowledge in the field of _____. My purpose in this profession is to help my customers to be more effective in manufacturing and marketing their products, so that they in turn can better serve their customers and provide opportunities for their employees. I enjoy my work and will be guided to say and do things that will contribute to my continued personal growth.

Those are my words. It's important that you choose words that are uniquely your own—that are especially meaningful to you. Compose several variations of your positive affirmations. Get in the habit of saying them with a good deal of deliberation in order to counteract any negative thoughts that would tend to creep in. Repeat your positive affirmation as you start your day, before you initiate a call, whenever you feel the need to boost your confidence.

The popular phrase "search for excellence" was inspired by the book *In Search of Excellence: Lessons From America's Best-Run Companies* by Thomas J. Peters and Robert H. Waterman, Jr. (New York: Harper & Row, 1982). The phrase connotes a philosophy espoused by Peters and Waterman and adopted by many organizations today. A common aspect of this discipline is to instill in members of the organization a sense of mission about why their organization exists. This mission is articulated in a mission statement.

Individuals who are in their own personal search for excellence actually do the same thing. They have a sense of mission about what they intend to do with their lives. And they articulate their mission in a personal mission statement.

Let your positive affirmation become your personal mission statement. It will certainly become an important self-motivator that will help you get rid of the fear of making cold calls.

What You Can Learn With Your Eyes Closed

There is another important way that ideas can be changed. For example, I will give you the word *beach*. Now put the book down for about thirty seconds and close your eyes.

What did you see in your mind's eye? White sand? A pounding surf? Sailboats in the distance? Sunbathers lying on beach blankets? Children making sand castles? A picture recalled from your own experience on a beach? Or did you picture the word B-E-A-C-H?

Most likely you pictured familiar scenes that the word *beach* evoked in your mind rather than the word. As important as words are in representing ideas, mental pictures are also important, sometimes more so. You can control the pictures that dwell in your mind as well as the words. For centuries philosophers have been telling us that we tend to act out the pictures we allow in our minds. Recently their philosophical musings have been proved in studies using scientific methods.

A Sure-Fire Method for Dissolving Fear

Despite their best efforts to do so, some salespeople have difficulty in avoiding images of hostile prospects. If you are affected this way, then it is best to make the image absurdly extreme.

One of my clients has an experienced field sales manager who is quite good at getting trainees to do this. Once, when the company was opening up a new territory. Ed Posnan was hired for his first sales job. Jack Davis, the manager, worked with Ed for two weeks before sending him out on his own. For the first week the older man did most of the work. He led Ed into likely businesses, introduced both of them to potential customers, and demonstrated the company line of building supplies. Jack made a good number of presentations, sold several new accounts, and laid a good foundation for Ed's follow-up calls. The young man watched, took many notes, and asked questions.

At the start of the second week, Jack instructed Ed to make a call by himself. He pointed out a factory that made prefabricated houses.

"This is the Thompson Company. I want you to go in, introduce yourself to Mr. Thompson, and present our line to him."

Ed gulped hard, stared at the building, but made no move.

"Tell me, Ed. Where are you now?"

The younger man looked confused by the question.

"Why, in your car in Thompson's parking lot."

"And what is the very worst thing that could happen if you call on Mr. Thompson today?"

Ed thought about that for a moment.

"I suppose he could swear at me for interrupting his work. He could refuse to hear my presentation. He might even have plant security escort me to the front door. I don't think they would throw me out bodily. Too much danger of a lawsuit in that these days."

Jack nodded thoughtfully. "And then where would you be?"

Ed started to laugh and then turned to get his case from the back seat.

"Right back here, sitting in your car in Thompson's lot."

"See?"

Ed laughed aloud and lifted his case from the back seat. "I think I'll go see if Thompson's security guards are all that tough."

The procedure that Jack used with Ed was a modification of the process taught by Dr. Viktor Frankl, a renowned Austrian psychiatrist. He calls it *paradoxical intention*.[3] It is based on the principle that the harder we try not to think about something, the more difficult it is to forget it.

In the Middle Ages, charlatans would sell lead bars to gullible peasants with the guarantee that they would change into gold overnight, providing the purchaser *did not* think about becoming wealthy. It was a perfect catch-22 proposition. No one could spend the night waiting for lead to become gold without gloating about the good fortune and anticipated wealth. In the morning when the lead had not changed, the charlatan would accuse the poor sucker of not following instructions. And the peasant would have to admit that he had, indeed, thought about becoming wealthy.

The harder we try not to think about fear, the more it comes unbidden to mind. On the other hand, it is possible to embrace the fear, turn it into a ridiculous affair, and allow the normal human appreciation of the absurd to turn it off completely.

When paradoxical intention is used in therapy, people are instructed to conjure up their worst fears rather than to avoid them. They are to embrace them, to magnify them greatly, and to make them so absurd that their minds rebel at the ridiculousness of the images being created. Paradoxical intention can be used as an inner conversation with oneself or in an actual conversation with someone else.

Ed Posnan might have said something like this:

> I am getting ready to face up to Old Man Thompson. I am terrified because he is the meanest human being in history. Beside him, Hitler, Genghis Khan, and Nero are all choirboys. He is so cruel that he hires guards with tommy guns to keep his employees from storming the office during coffee breaks.
>
> Along the back wall of his office, stuffed and mounted like hunting trophies, are the heads of former salespeople who called on him. Of the last 200 men and women who tried to sell him anything, only one got away to tell how mean Thompson really is. He is so bad that his secretary is the former karate champion of Japan. She can handle him but I can't be expected to.
>
> I'm really going to bomb out. When I get in there, I'm really going to make a fool of myself. I'll be standing there before him, looking at all those heads mounted along the wall behind his desk, and I'll turn to a quivering mass of protoplasm. My knees will shake and I'll stammer like a sophomore at my first dance. He'll snarl at me, the fire and smoke will come from his mouth, and I won't be able to say a word. I'll be stricken so mute that I'll never be able to speak again to another prospect, even if I somehow make it out of there before he cuts off my head.

Just try telling something like that to a friend with a straight face! The absurdity is so obvious that the human mind will immediately reject it. For if there is anything that our minds appreciate, it is the patently ridiculous. Harvard psychologist Gordon Allport wrote that any person who can devise a way to laugh at his problems is well on the way to solving them. Once ridiculed thoroughly, they lose the power to tie the mind in a helpless knot.

Norman Cousins was suffering unending agony from what was diagnosed as terminal cancer. He discovered, however, that he could end his pain at will by watching old Laurel and Hardy movies until he had a belly laugh. Each spasm of laughter would end his pain for half an hour or more.

The absurdity of a paradoxical intention statement, which would seem to make the problem worse, invariably has the opposite result. Hence the term paradoxical. It actually deflates a fear by opening it to ridicule and exposing it for the fraud the fear really is. The human mind cannot contain both the fear and the ridiculous image the paradoxical statement calls up to consciousness. After all, if you have faced the possibility of having your head handed to you on a platter, however jokingly, nothing a customer can actually do will be serious by comparison.

The ridicule of the paradoxical intention should be directed at the fear and not at yourself. If your anxieties are too strong to use the technique by yourself, have a trusted friend speak the absurdities for you.

Dr. Jard DeVille, author of *Nice Guys Finish First*, has had considerable experience using paradoxical intention as a mental health process. He says: "Don't let the apparent simplicity of the process keep you from using it, since it is one of the most powerful psychological techniques ever developed. I have seen many people rid themselves of a lifetime of phobias in a few minutes with it."[4]

A Plus Value—Growth

Even if you do not go to the extent of thinking up absurdities, consider the worst thing that could actually happen to you on a call. Whatever words or pictures you use to describe it, logic will not permit you to include someone slapping your face, or calling the police, or throwing you out bodily. The worst possible thing that could happen, as with Ed Posnan, is that you would be right back where you started. You didn't have any business from that prospect before going in. You don't have any coming out. Nothing lost but a few minutes' time and maybe a little injured pride.

Ask yourself what your objective is. Is it to avoid failure, or is it to achieve something significant? Is it to protect your ego, or is it to sell your product or service? Is it to maintain the status quo, or is it to gain valuable experience?

A baseball player often swings a leaded bat just before his turn at the plate. This makes the regular-weight bat seem easier by contrast. Likewise, if you get practice on tougher prospects and learn to deal with them effectively, the average ones will be a piece of cake.

As you gain more experience, your confidence will grow. It will become easier. You will eagerly look forward to more such experience. Selling becomes fun.

Success in your sales career is measured not only in immediate sales but also in your growing skill in being better able to deal with all kinds of situations. Rejection and injured pride are transient. They will pass. Personal growth is permanent. It can never be taken away from you.

This growth happens as the cumulative effect of experience, day after day, call after call. But sometimes it comes in a flash of insight from one experience in particular. That can be a real turning point in your career and that can be exciting. It happened to me.

How to Deal With a Tough Prospect

Years ago when I was selling radio advertising, and was the newest member of the station's sales staff, I was assigned a list of businesses to call that had previously spent very few dollars on radio advertising. One prospect was a crotchety old auto dealer who seemed to like to enliven dull afternoons by shaking up salespeople who came to call.

One afternoon he gave me a particularly rough going over.

I was thoroughly psyched out. The next thing I remember I was standing on the sidewalk in front of his dealership scratching my head.

"Hoo boy, there's got to be a better way to make a living," I thought.

It so happened I had had lunch a few hours earlier with a friend who told me a story that I now believe I was fated to hear that day. I really think that's the way it works. You get the help you need when you need it if you are immersed in what you're supposed to be doing.

Who Has the Problem?

The story concerned two businessmen who were in competition with each other. It was tough competitive business and they just hated each other's guts. Each had his office in the same tall building and every morning they would get on the elevator at the same time.

One was tall with a full head of hair. The other was short and bald. Every morning the tall one would stand behind the short one on the elevator and spit on his bald head. Every morning the short one would take a facial tissue out of his pocket and wipe his head off without saying a word.

A third man would also get on that elevator every morning at the same time. He watched this daily drama with a good deal of curiosity. After a couple of weeks he couldn't restrain his curiosity anymore.

"Tell me something, why do you let that guy get away with such a gross insult?" he asked the short man after the tall one got off the elevator to his lower-floor office.

"Well, you know that's his problem, not mine," the bald one replied.

Stop to think about that for a minute. When people are rude to us, even sometimes when they are unfair to us, it's really their problem, not ours. When we give them a taste of their own medicine, we're stooping to their level. It's better to pity people like that.

So there I was in front of this car dealership ready to throw in the towel and the meaning of that story jarred loose my self-pity. "Of course," I thought, "that car dealer has a problem, not me. He's sick, not me."

I recalled the days when I was a kid. The bully was never the toughest kid on the block. The bully acted that way because he was scared inside. It's the way he learned to keep other kids at a safe distance. Sometimes we see that bully behavior in a grownup. Psychologists tell us that such a person is the one who most fears rejection. Deep down he is timid. He adopts such obnoxious behavior in order to protect himself from the possibility of being hurt.

Unmasking the Toughness

But he does buy goods and services. He must, in order to keep his business functioning. Somebody is selling to him. Salespeople who sell to him don't mirror his unpleasantness. Nor do they come with hat in hand. In his heart the bully knows he has a weakness. Never mind how firmly he may deny it. In order to mask it, he will make a special effort to show his contempt for weakness in others.

Those who sell to him understand that beneath the mask of antagonism is another kind of person, one who can be sold. And they penetrate his hard shell with understanding, with patience, and with a firm belief in the value of what they sell.

You don't change people, but the relationship changes. I realized I couldn't change that crotchety car dealer, but I could change my perception of him. I did just that right there on the sidewalk by merely feeling sorry for him. Once a genuine feeling of pity sank in, my fear of him and others like him evaporated.

Psychologist Erich Fromm explains in his book *The Art of Loving* what happens during this kind of change of perception:

> I may know that a person is angry, but I may know him more deeply than that. Then I know that he is anxious and worried— that he feels lonely—that he feels guilty. Then I know that his

anger is only the manifestation of something deeper. I see him as anxious and embarrassed. That is as the suffering person, rather than the angry one.[5]

Now it didn't happen that I went back in and sold the car dealer a big contract. But there were others down through the years that I did successfully sell to. Lacking this newly gained insight, I might have been tempted to shy away from them. I surely would have hated to subtract those commissions from my earnings, to say nothing of the self-esteem that would have been surrendered along the way.

It pays to cultivate customers like Mr. Obnoxious. Once you get through to them, you have loyal customers.

Getting Rid of Irritation and Frustration

Robert Conklin, creator of the "Adventures in Attitudes" program and author of a best-seller on personal growth entitled *How to Get People to Do Things,* offered this insight in an earlier work, *The Dynamics of Successful Attitudes:* "We usually form opinions about how other people should act. Then we sit in constant judgment of them. Each time they do not conform to one of our molds, we pull the trigger of one of 5,000 irritations and frustrations."[6]

This means that the irritations, the frustrations, and the fears are self-imposed. We choose to activate them within ourselves. We could choose, instead, not to activate them, by tempering our judgments and by changing our perception. Then we would be much stronger emotionally to deal with the stresses in the sales profession.

If you ever have a prospect who is rude to you, who is unfair, who is out of line, simply pause a few seconds before you respond to the rudeness. Then ask this question:

"Ms. Prospect, have I offended you in any way?"

The fact is, unless you did something out of line, you didn't offend. Sometimes you catch prospects in a bad mood and they say something they really didn't mean to say. When you ask that question, it brings them back to reality. They realize they didn't mean to treat you rudely.

If you use the telephone to contact prospects, bear in mind the telephone is not a private network. It is a public utility! A listed phone number invites you to access that number. Anyone who wishes to deny such an invitation can get an unlisted number.

Suppose we had a dictator who declared, "Henceforth all surgery will be prohibited." What would happen? Those who needed surgery would be in trouble. And maybe the rest of us would worry that someday we would need it. But otherwise life would go on much the same.

Now suppose we had a dictator who declared, "All selling will be prohibited." Everybody's lifestyle would come to a screeching halt. Who is more important, doctors or salespeople?

Preparing a Solid Foundation

Whenever the stresses build up after a series of disappointments, read this chapter again. Ponder how the ideas suggested in it would apply to individual calls that you made. Put yourself into the situations of the salespeople in the examples. The ability to use your power of choice is a skill. As with any skill, it will improve with practice. Practice the technique of changing your mental words and pictures as suggested in this chapter until it becomes second nature. This will prepare a solid foundation to your complete strategy for developing new business. You will build on this foundation in the following chapters.

Chapter 3

WHAT DO YOU WANT TO HAPPEN?

"In a nutshell, I can tell you the difference between my top producers and the ones just getting by," a sales manager once told me. "My top producers are motivated by a desire for pleasing results. The mediocre ones are motivated by a desire for pleasing methods. And they will settle for whatever results their comfortable way of operating will bring."

It Begins With an End

The idea of setting objectives, of making clear-cut decisions on exactly what results you want, is not a new idea in personal motivation or in business or in selling in particular. You can hardly pick up a book on the subject of selling without a chapter on goal setting or attend a sales seminar where it isn't an important part of the agenda. If you've been in the sales profession for any length of time, chances are you've been

31

required to put in writing some kind of forecast of what you expect to accomplish.

This chapter is not intended to be a primer on the subject of goal setting. Rather, its purpose is to point out the importance of making clear-cut definitions of and commitments to exactly what we want to accomplish in getting new business.

People Resist Change

It is reasonable to assume you are reading this book in order to bring about a change that results in new business. To keep doing what you have been doing in the past will only bring the same results as in the past. In order to bring about a change in results, you must do things differently. This is not easy. Often those who want the benefits of change will resist doing what is necessary to make it happen.

I played the accordian years ago, back in the days when accordians were popular. In fact, I made a living at it for a while, but I don't play it much anymore. Occasionally, when we are entertaining friends, someone will insist I bring it out and play a few tunes.

"You must get a lot of enjoyment out of playing an instrument like that," somebody will usually remark.

"Matter of fact, I don't," is my standard reply. "I can't play it the way I used to. I know what the music is supposed to sound like. But I just can't make the fingers do it anymore."

"Lee, you're crazy not to play that accordian more often," a friend once said. "I'd give anything to play a musical instrument like that. You know, I've always wanted to play the guitar. I love to sing. So then I could sing and play the guitar, and that'd be great."

"Are you serious about that?" I asked.

"Of course I am."

"Well, consider it done." I gave him a sheet of paper and a pencil and said, "Now write this down: 'I will buy a guitar next week.' "

He wrote that down. "Now write this down: 'I will take lessons on this guitar starting next week.' "

He wrote that down. "Now this: 'I will practice playing that guitar thirty minutes a day starting next week.' "

After staring at his written words silently for several minutes, he crumpled up the sheet and threw it in the wastebasket.

Yes, there is a price to pay for bringing about change in one's life. Sometimes people are unwilling to pay it even though there can be a far greater price to pay for not changing. The choice must be made.

"A big mental health problem today is boredom," said one psychiatrist. "It's not the routine, which most people blame, that causes the boredom. It's the endlessness of what they are doing. They just never seem to arrive at any particular destination. They never seem to get anywhere simply because they don't know where they want to go." They are like Alice in Wonderland.

> "Would you tell me, please, which way I ought to go from here?"
> "That depends a good deal on where you want to get to," said the Cat.
> "I don't much care where—" said Alice.
> "Then it doesn't matter which way you go," said the Cat.[7]

Ridiculous, isn't it? And most people in the audience laugh at Alice when I tell that story in my seminars. It is ridiculous when you are talking about Alice in Wonderland. But it is tragic when you are talking about real people—and their lives.

The process of setting goals accomplishes a sifting through the choices. Most people never learn that process. They may hear or read about it, but they fail to assimilate the meaning of it in their own lives.

Going Through the Motions

People in an organization that is being managed by some sort of formalized goal-setting program resist the goal-setting discipline also. As a consultant, I'm occasionally called in to be a troubleshooter on a management by objectives program that isn't working too well. The first thing I look for is participants just going through the motions, that is, filling out forms because their boss expects it of them.

Just before the quarterly performance review, there is a scramble to find the forms, which had not been looked at since they were filled out. Then creative energy is spent thinking up excuses why the job wasn't done. There is no commitment to the completion of those objectives.

Believe in Setting Goals

In cases where the organizational goal-setting programs are working to good effect, I find commitment flourishing—not only a commitment to the stated objectives, but also a commitment to the concept of goal setting as a way of life. The participants believe in it. They apply the goal-setting procedures in their personal and family lives as well as on the job.

It is even more important for salespeople to apply this principle. They must be self-starters, self-motivated. They don't punch a time clock or have constant supervision. The principle of goal setting has special meaning in making new contacts if there is any resistance to change or fear of rejection. It is human nature to do what is pleasant and avoid doing what is not. Goals will keep you on course—keep you doing what is necessary for successful achievement regardless of whether or not you like the necessary activities. Goals will keep you from going off in directions you had not intended to go and wasting valuable time.

Goals are also essential to cold call selling because this phase of selling requires a good deal of creativity. Things must be made to happen from scratch!

The human brain is a super scanning device. When goals are clear, antennas go out. You will see and hear things that otherwise would be missed. The things you see and hear will have a different meaning as they apply to what you want to happen, and you will be able to make use of them.

The brain is also a super computer. Setting goals is the way it is programmed. Goals are the input. Creative ideas and solutions to problems are the output.

The wisdom underlying that concept is not particularly new. It was understood by King Hammurabi in ancient Babylon around 1750 B.C. At that time there was a problem with stone buildings collapsing and occupants getting killed. King Hammurabi put out an edict that declared, "If a building collapses and any occupant is killed, the builder will be put to death!" It is easy to imagine how creative the Babylonian builders became in figuring out how those buildings were to be built once they knew exactly what they had to achieve.

Three Elements Necessary for Change

Observations from my consulting practice and my training of thousands of salespeople and managers on the job have convinced me that change just does not take place without all three of these elements:

1. A clear definition of exactly what is to change
2. A firm commitment to make it happen
3. An action plan to carry it out

Defining a Goal

Here are vital points for defining a goal.

▪ 1. *Put it in writing.* We often think of writing as a means of communicating with other people. But what we write can be more enlightening to ourselves than to others. We can hold endless numbers of words in thought, but writing them down is a process of editing thoughts into their essential meaning. This avoids conflicting aims. If you choose to go north, you give up all possibility of going south for the time being.

Sometimes this is not clear until it is written. Writing also keeps us honest. We are less likely to kid ourselves in writing. Remember my friend who thought he wanted to play the guitar? When he wrote it down the truth came out. He was not willing to pay the price to learn.

▪ 2. *Quantify it.* Avoid vague statements such as, "My goal is to get some new business." You could get one new account that ordered a token amount of your product over a year's period of time and that goal, as stated, would have been achieved.

To make your goal statements positive affirmations, put them in the *past* tense, and quantify them: "To have sold twenty new accounts with total volume of $200,000." A quantified statement has numbers in it. Without numbers there is no way to recognize when the goal is achieved. The numbers also serve as measurements to check your progress. You can identify where you may need help or extra effort. The numbers also serve as a motivating force reminding you specifically of what it is you want to accomplish. The real world is brutally specific. Vague, wandering generalities just don't make contact with the real world.

▪ 3. *Date it.* Include in your goal statement the date you expect to achieve your goal. People resist doing this. It can be disturbing, even frightening—because it imposes a deadline responsibility for making it happen. Undated goals are meaningless. Not setting a time limit indicates a lack of decisiveness about reaching the goal. It is always off in some misty future. You are like the donkey with a carrot on the stick. It's always out there in front of you, but you never get to it.

A complete, written goal statement that is quantified and dated would read: "To have sold twenty new accounts with total volume of $200,000 by December 31." A written definition that is quantified and dated is a precondition for the next step.

Making the Commitment

Recently one of my clients had me fly to a sales meeting site in one of the company aircraft. To my surprise it was a single-engine plane.

"Isn't this unusual?" I asked the pilot. "I've flown in a lot of corporate aircraft and this is the first single-engine job I can recall." He replied:

Well, most people feel safer in a twin-engine plane. They figure if one engine quits, you have another one to keep you up. But consider this. It takes a lot more pilot skill to keep a twin-engine aircraft flying with one engine out. It's terribly unbalanced. It's especially tough in bad weather. Worse, if you have to make a forced landing in bad weather.

But pilot skill is only part of it. The real reason you may want to consider a single-engine airplane safer is this. If that engine quits, the pilot is totally committed to land that bird. There is no other option. Total attention, skill, and effort are concentrated on bringing it down as gently as possible. No distractions.

A twin-engine pilot, no matter how skilled, isn't applying all of that skill to the one critically important task. A twin-engine pilot's mind is going back and forth struggling with a dilemma. Should I keep it up? Should I bring it down?

It occurred to me that people go through life like that. They never make a clear-cut decision—a commitment, so they can concentrate all of their energy, attention, and skill on it.

Commitment casts aside the self-imposed barriers encountered in making new contacts, such as procrastination and fear of rejection. It activates the inner creative mechanism that penetrates and resolves prospect resistance. It thus drives a person to a level of attainment beyond that which could ordinarily be expected from previously demonstrated ability.

A written definition that is quantified and dated is a precondition for commitment. One doesn't become committed to vague ideas. First, make a decision of exactly what it is you want to happen. Then make a second decision expressed here as inner dialog.

Say to yourself with meaning and conviction, "Yes, this is what I am going to do." That is the essence of commitment.

Preparing Action Plans

Although goals are the source of motivating power, their realization does not happen automatically. They must be followed up with an action plan. Action plans translate goals into a step-by-step blueprint telling how the goals will be reached.

Salespeople are not inclined to be avid planners. For one thing, they are likely to be extroverts, and extroverts don't like routine. Planning is routine. Then too, plans have a way of being aborted. You make plans for a day when one of your biggest customers calls with a problem. You drop your carefully made plans to put out a brush fire. Other emergencies happen frequently. But all the reasons you hear from salespeople about why they can't plan are actually reasons why they should plan.

Planning is often referred to as time management. I've never particularly liked the term *time management* because we really can't manage time. The clock ticks on relentlessly and nothing that we can do will change its precise, measured progression. We can manage only ourselves. I believe the reason that so many of us are lacking in self-management skills is that we never got into the habit of practicing such skills early. Most of us began our working careers in a job at which we were paid by the hour. And to reinforce the abandonment of our self-management, we punched a time clock.

The time clock then became a very important center of attention. It managed us. It determined the design of our day. It determined the size of our paycheck. Punch in, punch out—the number of hours on the time card times the hourly rate was it. For the most part, the power to decide what we would get done while we were there was given to someone else. Our only responsibility was to be there. Punch in, punch out. We got paid, regardless. We developed a mental habit of thinking about our job as a block of time to be filled with activities. These activities would then satisfy the time clock requirements, which justified our paycheck and our value to the organization that paid us. We tended to focus on activities rather than results.

In the sales profession, responsibility for results shifts to the salesperson. This includes responsibility for planning how to make the results happen.

The Key Fundamental—Priorities

There are many excellent books, courses, and programs on planning, or time management. Although each may suggest different methods, they all have a common key element. That has to do with some method of identifying and setting priorities.

People usually have more things they would like to do or feel they ought to do than they have time to do. So they must choose. To set priorities is to make choices. If you live in Chicago and choose to go to New York, you give up all possibility of going to Los Angeles at the same time. That is obvious. It is also a hypothetical situation. But without planning, we often place ourselves in similar incongruous situations in real life.

How to Determine Priorities—Force Field Analysis

A logical method for determining priorities is known as force field analysis. First, write out your goal statement at the top of a sheet of paper. Draw a line down the center. On the left-hand side directly under the goal statement write the words *Helping Forces*. On the right-hand side similarly write the words *Hindering Forces*. Now on the left-hand side write everything you can think of that is helping you to achieve the goal. For example, it could be strong personal characteristics you have, advantages your product has over competitors', people you work with, sales aids your company provides. Do some creative brainstorming and write down anything you can think of that could help you reach your goal. Keep writing as long as the ideas flow.

Now on the right-hand side write down all the things you can think of that prevent you from achieving the goal. The completed form would look something like Figure 1. Write them down as they occur to you. At this stage there is no need to list them in order of importance. Explore your feelings, especially those that would go under hindering forces. Be honest with this. To deny emotional reasons that hinder you from achieving your goal does not stop their hidden,

Figure 1. Force field analysis.

Goal: To have sold 20 new accounts with total volume of
$200,000 by December 31.

Helping Forces	*Hindering Forces*
1. Strong desire to achieve this goal.	1. Feel uncomfortable making new calls.
2. Territory with good potential.	2. Competitors are deeply entrenched.
3. Products with the following competitive advantages: a. b. c. d.	3. Our prices generally higher than competition's.
4. Benefits to the customer: a. b. c. d.	4. Have been unable to reach key buying authority in high-potential accounts.
5. Visual sales aids.	5. Servicing present customers is time-consuming and doesn't allow much time for new prospect calls.
6. Good advertising support.	
7. Supportive sales manager.	
8. Curiosity: I'm the new kid on the block!	

damaging effect. Just to admit them in writing so you can face them squarely will help to neutralize them.

After completing your list of helping forces and hindering forces, write your goal statement at the top of another sheet of paper. Draw a line down the center. On the left-hand side write, "What I can do to maximize the helping forces." On the right-hand side write, "What I can do to minimize the hindering forces."

Once again do some creative brainstorming and fill in each appropriate column with as many things as you can think of that would enable you to increase the positive effect of the helping forces and decrease the negative effect of the hindering forces.

You can do this exercise alone or with the help of your sales manager or another salesperson. It makes an excellent project for a sales meeting. Apply the rules of creative brainstorming. Aim for the largest quantity of ideas. As they flow, just write them down without making any judgments as to whether or not they are practical. Even silly ones can trigger your imagination for more useful possibilities. Use as many sheets for this as necessary.

Keep writing until you are reasonably sure your creative capacity is exhausted; then you can switch from the unrestricted, creative frame of mind to a judgmental one. Go back over your lists and refine them. Cross out the suggestions that are unusable. Narrow the lists down to essential items and arrange items in some order of importance. This can be done by assigning numbers to them or by arranging them in clusters, labeling each cluster A, B, or C according to its relative importance. Your Force Field Analysis is now complete. From this analysis you move on to the next step: developing a master action plan.

The Master Action Plan

The master plan is a list of subgoals, in order of priority, of all the things that need to get done in order to achieve the main goal. Figure 2 is an example of such a plan. Notice that

Figure 2. Master action plan.

Goal: To have sold 20 new accounts with total volume of
$200,000 by December 31.

1. Sell one new account each week, with average sale of
   $10,000 projected for balance of the year.
2. Make 5 presentations to new prospects each week.
3. Add 10 new prospects to list each week.
4. List all accounts and prospective accounts in order
   of priority (to be completed by 8/10).
5. Set up itinerary geographically and in proportion to
   account priority (to be completed by 8/15).
6. Write out telephone opening script (to be completed
   by 8/16).
7. Compose precall letter (to be completed by 8/17).
8. Send 10 precall letters each week (beginning 8/19).

once again the goal statement is written out at the top to keep
the original goal clearly in mind. Only eight items are shown
in Figure 2 to show the form the master plan would take. It's
likely you would have more items based on the final draft of
your Force Field Analysis. The number in front of each item
indicates relative priority.

The master plan provides a basis for your daily action plan.
This is a list, again in order of priority, of the things you
expect to get done that day. Notice the term "to get done"
instead of "to do." Many people make up "to do" lists every
day. "To do" lists are certainly better than no plan at all. But,
the "to do's" tend to be activities, not end results. For
example, making a call is an activity. Making a sale is an end
result. Express your list in terms of end results rather than
activities—a "to get done" list instead of a "to do" list. Like
the builders of ancient Babylon, you will discover how creative you will be in figuring out what you need to do in order
to accomplish what you want to get done. Get into the mental
habit of thinking in terms of end results rather than being
satisfied with filling your day with busywork.

There will be days when you will only finish one or two items on your lists. That's OK. If you start from the top of the lists, take heart from the fact that you are working on the highest priorities. The others will just have to wait. You may not get all the things done you would like to by this method, but it wouldn't be possible to get them done at all any other way. If you don't have a method of consciously and deliberately committing your time to what you choose to be your highest priorities, it is most likely you will subconsciously gravitate toward doing what is more pleasing, less risky, less difficult but also less important, less productive, less rewarding.

If all of this sounds like extra work, I would ask compared with what? At first glance it may seem to be extra work compared with no planning at all. But good planning does not increase the workload. Instead, it helps you to work more effectively and productively with less physical effort. A salesperson who doesn't plan is like the man chopping wood with a dull axe!

"Why don't you sharpen your axe?" a friend asked.

"I can't take the time to stop. It's taking me long enough to do this job as it is."

Ridiculous? Of course. But no more ridiculous than to launch into a day of selling without a clearly thought out plan of action. Do your planning during off hours—evenings or early in the morning before your selling day begins.

Some people fail in selling because of lack of product or technical knowledge. But many more people fail because they don't put the knowledge they have to profitable use. This is not to say that product knowledge isn't important. It is. It's like a hunting license. It gives you the right to your prospect's time and attention. But just as a hunting license doesn't make you an expert marksman, product knowledge doesn't give you everything you need to effectively sell the product.

So often, among the top sales leaders on my clients' sales teams, I find persons with less than average formal education. They succeed because they know what they want to achieve, are committed to reaching their goal, have a game plan, and spend their time on their high priorities.

Chapter 4

WHERE TO FIND PROSPECTS

Some years ago I was engaged in hiring and training people to sell a sales training service to business firms. We would hire only one person in a given territory, selected carefully on the basis of a proven set of criteria. When more than one candidate met these criteria, some of my personal bias would color the final decision. I leaned toward someone who showed a lot of enthusiasm for the program we were selling and who would seem to enjoy selling it. Usually those characteristics added a plus factor that would help a newcomer start off successfully.

Jim Tucker checked out as an ideal candidate. He was a likable, intelligent young man who was quick to grasp the merit of our program. "This business is made to order for me. It's just what I've been looking for. I can't wait to get going on my own."

I kept hearing these and similar remarks during the first two days of my initial field training with him. It was a straight commission sales job with no salary or draw provided, so these remarks were nice to hear. Often a trainee's attitude would have a touch of "OK, show me it can be done." But Jim showed more eagerness and enthusiasm than most other trainees I had worked with.

The first two days were spent following up leads provided by Art Anderson, the recently retired territory salesperson. After a quick lunch Wednesday noon, I took Jim to the public library to show him how to use various directories to identify prospects. Wednesday evening we went back to the library for a couple of hours to dig up more prospects.

I impressed upon Jim the importance of using the hours between eight o'clock in the morning and noon and between one o'clock and five o'clock in the afternoon to be in contact with prospects.

"These are the golden selling hours," I told him. "The hours when prospects are available are the only hours that pay off in commissions. Paperwork, library work, and planning are most profitably done at other times."

Jim was more quiet than usual as we drove from the library back to my hotel that evening. I guessed he was digesting all my sage advice.

The next morning when I awoke, the message light on my phone was blinking.

"Good morning, Mr. Boyan. There is an envelope in your box," was the cheery greeting from the hotel desk clerk. Here is what it said:

Dear Lee:

I will be unable to continue as a representative for your firm. I was called out of town for an important personal matter. I am sorry this happened. Thank you for your patience and your help.

Sincerely,
Jim Tucker

Beyond Enthusiasm

Several weeks passed before I was able to reach Jim by phone. It took a little probing before Jim finally admitted that he just couldn't see himself spending all that time digging through directories.

"I sincerely believe that you have the best program of its kind and one that is much needed by many companies. I wish I had used such a program when I first started my selling career. Your method of presenting it is just super, something I'd enjoy doing. But, Lee, the detail involved in looking up prospects kinda got to me." This was Jim's wistful parting shot.

Jim's case may be somewhat extreme. Reason would suggest that if he were as enthusiastic about the program and its presentation as he claimed to be, a certain amount of detail work would be endured in good spirits. But often people don't behave reasonably. There is a little bit of Jim in many salespeople when it comes to the nonselling detail work involved.

The first step in making a sale is finding someone to sell to. At first glance this may seem obvious, but the best way to do it may not be readily apparent. In some selling situations, the prospects are easily identified. For example, a manufacturer of certain mechanical or electronic components would have a limited number of original equipment manufacturers who would have use for such components. The OEM prospects most likely would be well known in their trade. Companies that sell through a dealer or distributor organization may only occasionally need to replace or add customers. Dealers handling their products are easily spotted in the Yellow Pages of the phone book.

Become Prospect-Minded

For most salespeople, however, prospecting is a never-ending search in less conspicuous places. Gary Flaherty sells sales incentive and premium merchandising programs to business firms. He enjoys a very high income and is tops in his field. When I asked him what single factor he felt contributed the most to his success, Gary explained:

I'm not smarter than anybody. In fact I have only one year of college and didn't do too well there at that. And I'm not what you'd call a hard worker, but when I work, I want to spend that working time with the best prospects I can find. Now in order to do this I spend more time thinking about prospecting than any other phase of my job. The more I think about prospects the more good ones seem to turn up for me.

Here is a valuable lesson from a successful pro. Like Gary, become prospect-minded. Realize the importance of prospecting. Include in your action plans some time to develop and maintain a workable prospect file.

Suspects or Prospects

Prospecting is often thought of as the actual contact of potential customers, but before that can happen the potential customers must be identified. The act of simply accumulating names sometimes is referred to as suspecting. True prospecting involves gathering specific information that gives some indication of the likelihood that an individual or organization would be a buyer of your product or service. If you sell to business firms, the size of a company in terms of its annual sales or number of employees could tell you whether or not it is worth your time to make a call, because that information would tell you something about sales volume potential for your products there. Credit rating speaks for itself. Names of key individuals along with their titles give clues to where the buying authority may be. Other information will suggest which of your products or services can best satisfy their needs and how to approach them. A prospect, then, may be defined as someone who needs what you sell, can afford it, and has authority to buy.

If you sell direct to individuals or to families, you may have to devote more time to prospecting. In this case just getting names of suspects is easy. Any telephone book can give you all the names you want. But getting prospects with some degree of qualification is quite another task. Here your best source of prospects is from referrals from satisfied customers.

How to Get Referrals

Satisfied customers are your best sources of referrals. The key word here is *satisfied*. The more satisfied your customers are, the higher the quality of leads you will get from them. Opportunities for giving customers satisfaction are great in direct selling because typically customers are not accustomed to having their satisfaction assured.

Think back over major purchases you have made of personal or household items such as automobiles, furniture, appliances, insurance, or remodeling work. Do you recall any time the salesperson came back after the sale was made to see if everything was satisfactory? Not too often, I'll bet. How do you feel about that?

On the other hand, how would you feel toward a salesperson who did come back to see how well you were getting along with the investment you made? Suppose the salesperson gave you some ideas on how to make the greatest use of the product or how to take good care of it or otherwise showed genuine concern for your maximum satisfaction. Wouldn't you be more inclined to help that salesperson find other people who would be given similar care and concern for their satisfaction?

Yes, making after-the-sale follow-up and service calls is time wisely invested. Most salespeople in the direct specialty field don't do it because of a mistaken notion that it is unproductive to do so. After all, the customer has already bought, and for a nonrepeat product, it is unlikely that the customer will buy again for a while. And if the customer really isn't satisfied, all too many salespeople would rather avoid that confrontation. Yet, they should be the first to know if there is any kind of problem so it can be taken care of. Otherwise, the whole neighborhood and other acquaintances of the customer are likely to hear about it and be forever lost as prospects for the salesperson.

Referrals are also an excellent source of prospects for selling to business firms, institutions, and government units. Service calls are equally important in these markets. The nature of products and services sold to this sector usually requires more follow-up calls, especially when repeat sales are a possibility. But for the very reason that follow-up calls happen here more often, salespeople frequently overlook the opportunity to ask for referred leads.

Persons of buying authority in the business and professional world maintain close contact with others of similar interest through trade and professional associations, service clubs, and other affinity groups. Be aware of these networks and of the opportunities they provide to add high-quality prospects to your file.

Please take special note of the words *high-quality*. You don't want just names, you want names of the best prospects that your customer can give. So before you ask for referrals it is important to get your customer into a frame of mind that is conducive to giving you the best possible names. First make sure your customer is completely satisfied. Ask a few questions regarding how the product is being used or about comments of other people involved with it. Of course, you are open to hearing a complaint or a problem, because if there is any dissatisfaction, what chance would you have of getting a good referral? On the other hand, here you are ready, willing, and eager to help your customer solve the problem.

Most likely there is no problem and you have a customer who is satisfied. Expand that satisfaction. Offer suggestions for even greater satisfaction. Ask questions about what it is that customer likes most about the product, the service, or dealing with you and your company. Try to get the customer's own words about a specific benefit. Often in the enthusiastic recounting of benefits the customer will volunteer names of others who should be enjoying the same benefits. But if not, now is the time to suggest there may be acquaintances of your customer who are missing out on those benefits. Or tell a story of another customer of yours who was struggling without the benefits until you came along and showed a better way. Make it clear that you are dedicated to helping people solve problems and there are, no doubt, a lot of people out there who could use your help.

Ordinarily, when a salesperson asks for referrals it sounds something like this: "Now that you are my customer, would you help me sell more of my product? I would appreciate the names of acquaintances of yours who would be prospects for me."

But you're going to be different. Your first order of business is helping others instead of yourself. Your emphasis and concern is not on selling products but on solving problems, on making life and business better for the friends of your customer. You are going to give those people the same kind of care and concern you have just demonstrated on that follow-up call. Now the customer is in the proper frame of mind to give serious thought to who would be the very best prospects for you and is more eager to make extra effort to help you contact these high-quality prospects.

Know Who You Are Looking For

It is important to develop a profile of your best prospect. Make a list of your best customers. Study this list. Look for the characteristics they have in common. When asking for referrals mention these characteristics to help the referrer think of names of people who match your profile. Be aware of those characteristics in all of your prospecting efforts. Some of the highest-paid salespeople such as Gary Flaherty are simply good qualifiers. They want to spend their selling time where it pays off most.

Referrals are an ideal source of prospects but by no means the only source. The highest expression of skill in selling is demonstrated in the ability to make effective contact with unknown prospects or with whatever knowledge is available through published reference data. If you depend entirely on referrals, you probably are not making the most profitable use of the best hours in the day for selling because there will be times you'll find yourself in certain locales with time to spare but no one to call on. An adequate supply of fresh prospects in your files will help you turn otherwise wasted time into profit. Here are some good places to find them.

Primary Sources of Prospects

Dun's Marketing Services
Three Century Drive
Parsippany, NJ 07054

Million Dollar Directory, Volumes I, II, and III
   Provides detailed information on 160,000 of the largest businesses in the United States, including headquarters locations, names of key executives, number of employees, and sales volume. Listings are shown alphabetically, geographically, and by product Standard Industrial Classification (SIC) code number.

Billion Dollar Directory
   Complements the *Million Dollar Directory* by identifying U.S. ultimate parent companies having large corporate families. Shows corporate family linkage and ownership of subsidiaries and divisions. In-depth corporate family listings appear alphabetically, geographically, and by SIC code number. These are supplemented by an extensive cross-reference index of divisions, subsidiaries, and ultimate parent companies.

Dun's Business Identification Service
   Information on over 7.4 million U.S. business establishments listed on microfiche cards. Each listing includes name of company, address, and headquarters or branch designation.
   Dun's Marketing Services also publishes a metalworking industry directory, international directories, and other market profile analyses.

Dun & Bradstreet Corporation
49 Old Bloomfield Road
Mountain Lakes, NJ 07046

Dun's Electronic Yellow Pages
Separate databases include description of business; population of
city; number of employees; and whether a chain, headquarters, or
branch. It covers 7.5 million businesses. All available on computer-
readable formats, three-by-five-inch cards, or printouts.

Contacts Influential
9 Campus Drive
Parsippany, NJ 07054

Contacts Influential publishes directories of businesses in major
metropolitan markets. The information provided includes size of
company; whether a local, branch, or head office; length of time in
business; SIC code numbers; and key people. The directories are
updated monthly with new businesses, changes of ownership,
moves, rumored moves, and personnel changes. All of the information is computerized so special selections can be made for specific
types of accounts. For example, suppose you are in the insurance
business and want to contact the small-group market—companies
that have between six and fifty employees. Additionally, you don't
want branch offices because you can't get approval from a branch.
You don't want your competitors to know what you are doing so
you want to delete other insurance companies. Contacts Influential
can provide you with mailing labels for your mailing, three-by-five-
inch cards for follow-up, and a printout for a control factor of just
the companies you want.

Cole Publications
901 West Bond Street
Lincoln, NE 68521

City Cross-Reference Directory
Provides detailed information in several categories.
 1. Street Address Directory shows names of telephone subscri-
    bers listed by street address.

2. Numerical Telephone Directory shows name of each telephone subscriber according to the telephone number and whether it is a business or residence.
3. Office Building Directory shows names, titles, and occupations of tenants in each office building.
4. City and Suburban Newcomer list shows new listings and new arrivals.
5. Family Income Level and Buying Power Guide shows average wealth and ratings on each street.
6. Census Tract Marketing Section shows census tract maps of the entire area, including street guide, counts, and wealth rating for each tract.
7. Zip Code Marketing Section shows zip codes for the entire area, including street guides and counts for each zip code.
8. Demographic Section enables you to select trade areas by median age, median number of persons per household, percentage of owner-occupied households, percentage of families with children under twelve, median years of school completed, and a housing unit analysis.

Thomas Publishing Company
1 Penn Plaza
New York, NY 10119

Thomas Register of American Manufacturers
Lists 120,000 manufacturing companies alphabetically according to the products or services they manufacture. Two volumes list companies alphabetically by name with address, zip code, phone number, branch offices, capital rating, and key executives. A brand name index is also included. Six volumes are catalogs of companies.

Standard & Poor's Corporation
25 Broadway
New York, NY 10004

Register of Corporations, Directors and Executives
Lists 45,000 corporations and 400,000 officers, directors, and other principals, including an annual obituary listing and a separate listing of new individual and company additions.

R. L. Polk and Company
431 Howard Street
Detroit, MI 48231

Polk's City Directories
In addition to all large cities, Polk's series includes cities somewhat smaller than those included in the directories mentioned above. The directories identify occupations of some individuals and key executives of companies in the alphabetical section. A street address section lists principal occupants of each building, apartment, and office suite.

National Register Publishing Company
3004 Glenview Road
Wilmette, IL 60091

Standard Classified and Geographical Directories
Both directories list 17,000 companies with annual appropriations for national or regional advertising campaigns, approximate annual sales, approximate number of employees, type of products sold, and key executives. The classified directory arranges companies in fifty-one product categories. The geographical directory arranges them by state and city. A trade name list identifies companies when only the trade name is known.

Directory of Corporate Affiliations
Shows the corporate structure of major U.S. companies: their divisions, subsidiaries, and affiliates, both domestic and foreign.

Prospector Research Services, Inc.
751 Main Street
Waltham, MA 02154

Sales Prospector
A newsletter giving information on new companies and company expansions and relocations. Regional geographic editions.

Office of Procurement and Technical Assistance
Small Business Administration
1414 L Street N.W.
Washington, DC 20416

U.S. Government Purchasing and Sales Directory
   Lists the needs of the various government offices divided into military and nonmilitary spending.

Directory Service Company
950-52 South Sherman Street
Longmont, CO 80501

Rural Resident and Plat Directory
   Publishes county residence directories for finding prospects in rural areas. A map of each township is included showing who lives where.

Standard Rate and Data Service
3004 Glenview Road
Wilmette, IL 60091

   Two volumes of over 500 pages with over 50,000 consumer and business mailing lists used in direct mail advertising will give you the source of lists of almost any classification of prospect you can imagine. SRDS also publishes directories of radio stations, TV stations, newspapers, business publications, and consumer publications.

John Wiley & Sons, Inc.
605 Third Avenue
New York, NY 10158

Directory of Federal Purchasing Offices
   A listing of 130,000 government purchasers. Sections include agencies classified in groups by types of goods and services most frequently purchased, organization charts for all federal agencies,

geographical listings identifying local purchasing offices, and a glossary of abbreviations and acronyms.

Other Sources of Prospects

Phone book Yellow Pages are always handy. Most states publish directories of manufacturers and other businesses. Chambers of commerce usually have rosters of local businesses. Some large-city industrial directories classify businesses by zip code, which helps you confine prospecting to a limited geographical area and reduce wasted travel time. Local, regional, and national business magazines as well as the business section of local newspapers are excellent sources of information regarding personnel changes, new businesses, relocations, and expansions. Corporate annual reports are readily available that give in-depth information on key target prospects. Many industries, institutions, and organizations have nationwide directories. Trade and professional associations publish rosters of their memberships. Some trade magazines publish annual directory issues. Some sell their subscriber mailing lists.

If a source of information for your market has not been mentioned yet or you want to explore more possibilities, try this one:

Gale Research Company
Book Tower
Detroit, MI 48226

Directory of Directories
A reference guide of over 5,100 entries listing business and industrial directories, professional and scientific rosters, and all kinds of lists and guides. It lists 2,100 specific subject headings with cross-references. Detailed information about each directory should enable you to make a decision about the probable usefulness or application of each publication.

Many of the resources listed here are available in the reference department of public libraries. Reference desk librarians are usually eager to help you. After all, that is how they gain fulfillment and satisfaction from their job. One in particular, I recall, keeps a sign on her desk that says, "Disturb me a little . . . or a lot."

Mail List Brokers

Mail list brokers maintain and rent mailing lists sorted by business, profession, location, and several other specifications.

Computers and word processors have vastly changed the state of the art of compiling and maintaining lists. If you have data processing equipment available, you may be able to purchase software with prospect lists ready to go. With sophisticated programming, lists can be merged or purged to further narrow them to a precise qualification. Here is where a specific profile of your best customer is most helpful. The computer can be programmed to retrieve only names matching your profile.

If you don't have data processing available, a good mail marketing firm can keep you up to date with the state of the art. Trade publications of the direct mail business such as *Direct Mail Marketing* and *Zip* make interesting reading and offer many tips. Never mind that you may not be in the direct mail business. The professionals in that business are masters at compiling and maintaining prospect lists. You can learn much from their experience.

Everybody Is a Source of Leads

Your acquaintances can provide you with good leads. Everyone you know or contact in any way, especially people who consider you their customer, are lead generators. Let them know what business you are in and that you are looking for business. Every chance you get, ask the question: "Who do you know that is looking for a good buy in [your product or service]?''

Occasionally in my seminars when I discuss the idea of getting leads from friends or business contacts, sometimes called *radiation,* one or two people in my audience say that they would be hesitant to do that because it would be taking advantage of a friendship or other connection. My stock answer to that is, "Does your auto mechanic feel embarrassed talking about fixing cars?" "Does your clothier hesitate to talk about fashions?" It usually makes the point.

Be active in trade or professional associations, service organizations, and community projects. The more active the better. Get involved. Be willing and eager to do favors for people. Noncompeting salespeople calling on the same clientele are excellent sources; cultivate their friendship. Form networks with salespeople in your business in other parts of the country and exchange information. For my clients who have national distribution, I suggest a "Help Each Other Memo," which is a standard form for salespeople in different parts of the country and the world to share lead information.

When making a call on a business firm, you often sit in the reception lobby for a while waiting until the person you are calling on is ready to see you. Most likely there are trade publications, house organs, company directories, and annual reports available especially for waiting visitors. Such publications are loaded with prime prospecting information. Here is an opportunity to turn otherwise unproductive time into profitable prospecting time.

Fairs and Trade Shows

Fairs and trade shows offer a unique opportunity to get leads, qualify prospects, and even close sales. A survey by the Trade Show Bureau determined that 57 percent of trade show attendees are looking for new products and services. It's a safe bet that most of the rest are at least looking for a chance to learn about what is new in their field of interest. They are top-level decision makers who buy or whose recommendations are respected. Besides, they are not as preoccupied with other matters as they might be on a typical sales call. You just can't beat that for opportunity, but it requires alertness to capitalize on it fully.

I am often a guest speaker or seminar presenter at a trade convention. I make a special effort to spend some time at the exhibits to learn more about my clients' business. It's a great source of ideas that enables me to customize my presentation for the specific concerns of the audience.

In some booths I see attendants enthusiastically engaged in conversation with delegates, making things happen. Others sit quietly, sometimes even looking bored and expecting passers-by to initiate a conversation or at least pick up some literature.

One of the smartest operators I ever saw was Bob Komasinski. He would ask each passer-by a simple five-word qualifying question that immediately told him whether or not he had a good prospect. It was a concrete industry convention. Bob sells equipment used by manufacturers of ready-mix concrete. The question was, "How much do you pour?" The more concrete they poured, the more equipment they used, and the more Bob was able to sell them.

The first time I walked past Bob I replied. "I don't pour concrete but I pour words out of my mouth. I'm the keynote speaker tomorrow morning." Bob smiled, introduced himself and said. "Hey, I'll be there listening." Then he turned his attention to the person walking behind me and asked, "How much do you pour?"

Later on I had a chance to chat with Bob away from his booth and complimented him on his heads-up technique. Bob said:

I love conventions. I love people. I wish I could meet everybody here and get to know them better. There is a kind of carnival atmosphere to that exhibit floor that I have to separate my head from. It takes a certain amount of mental conditioning and discipline for me to do that. I'm not here just for the fun and excitement. This is a working day for me. One of the most

important of the year. I'm here to sell that equipment. I just
hope people passing my booth who are not prospects understand that and are not offended if I'm a little quick with them.

Yes, Bob Komasinski is right. Selling at trade shows is not for
fun seekers or for timid souls. It can be exhausting 16-hour
days. Hangovers and lack of sleep can ruin one of the best
selling days of the year.

You can increase traffic to your booth if you do some
preshow promotion. Get a list of advance registrants from the
show producers. Send them a letter or promotion piece offering a free gift, an idea, or some particular reason to visit your
booth. Like Bob Komasinski, be ready with effective qualifying questions to identify your best prospects. Above all, take
the initiative to meet attendees. Your best prospects will walk
right past your booth if you let them.

Always Be Looking

In addition to all the above-mentioned sources of finding
prospects, be sure to include just plain observation. In days
gone by this was known as *smokestacking*. For those who
sold to industry, where there was a smokestack, there was
potential business. Today the smokestack may well be re-
placed by a modern office building, but the concept of
smokestacking, which simply meant being observant, is still
sound. The outward appearance of a building, a name on the
door may be a "smokestack" for you. Look for any new
piece of construction, an unfamiliar sign on a building, or
remodeling in progress. Don't drive by and wonder; step in
and find out! An early call on the occupant may give you a
jump on competitors. Perhaps the occupant is new to the area.
This gives you an opportunity to build early goodwill by
offering to help with information based on your familiarity
with the locale.

It's a good idea to take alternative routes occasionally on
your way to established customers to see whether anything
new is going on in your territory. New office buildings are

constantly going up, some in newly developed outlying areas. Industrial parks located near limited access highways are often growing and changing. They are easily reached and provide a concentration of prospects if you sell to a variety of businesses. They are especially good places to work early in the morning and late in the afternoon, when traffic clogs the main roads in a metropolitan area.

Many people who I knew were unsuccessful in their attempt to establish a career in selling thought that it didn't pay to make prospect calls before nine-thirty in the morning or after three-thirty in the afternoon, because traffic makes it impossible to get around. It always amazed me why it didn't occur to them to use that time of the day in a concentrated area off the beaten track or in a downtown area where they could park the car and walk. Perhaps they really wanted to fail.

Another advantage to working a concentrated area is that it is an easy and quick way to get the kind of qualifying precall information that separates suspects from prospects. Whenever you make a call, whether an established customer or prospect call, ask questions about other tenants in the vicinity. Often receptionists are good sources. They are accustomed to giving information to strangers, and if they've been at that location for any length of time, they are familiar with their neighborhood.

Keep Good Records

It is important to have a convenient method of filing and retrieving prospect information. Computers are great, but even if you have access to data processing you need some method to record information as you gather it, and to carry it with you as you move about the territory. Make it a habit to write down information as soon as you get it, preferably on the same form you use when making calls. Unless you need to record a lot of detail information, three-by-five-inch or four-by-six-inch cards are best. They are easily filed and carried. By developing your own abbreviation code you can store a surprising amount of information on them.

A geographical file is most helpful. Whenever you plan to work a certain area, take the entire file of prospects for that locality. Even though your plans may be to work by appointment, you can put any open time to profitable use by making some prospect calls in that locality after consulting your geographical file. This way your prime selling time will be booked solidly, giving you many opportunities to put business on the books that otherwise might have been missed.

Get Full Territory Coverage

As I conduct needs analysis studies for clients, I find salespeople need training in how to get maximum coverage of their territories. Too often they are merely high-spotting the prospects who are easy to find. That's OK for the type of direct sales in which almost anybody can be a prospect, but getting only a fraction of the potential business out of a territory with limited clientele makes one a liability to oneself and to the company. It is interesting how often a new salesperson will take over a territory and immediately double the previous business. Most of the additional business comes from prospects who were not being called on. The new salesperson does a more thorough job of prospecting.

Remember Gary Flaherty, who credited his success to the fact that he spent a good deal of time thinking about prospects. High on your "to get done" list include adding a specific number of new prospects. You can't sell them if you don't know who they are.

Chapter 5

WHY SHOULD PROSPECTS LET US INTO THEIR WORLD?

A young man went to see the wise man on the hill to find out the secret of success.

"Go over to the window, look out, and tell me what you see," the wise man told him.

"I see the marketplace," the youth replied.

"Now go look into the mirror over there and tell me what you see."

"Well, naturally, I see myself."

"In each case you were looking through a pane of glass. Tell me, what is the difference?" the wise man asked.

"The window is a clear pane of glass that allows me to see out and see the people in the marketplace. The mirror has a backing of silver that reflects my image."

"Ah, son. Therein lies the secret of success: When you let silver come between you and the people in the marketplace, you are going to see only yourself."

The marketplace is full of people with all kinds of problems and with all kinds of needs. They especially need counsel, guidance, and professional expertise in finding solutions to problems of vital interest to them and in making choices to fulfill their needs.

Reread the story about Fred Hawkins in Chapter 2, especially the part where Fred said the most important sale he made was when he sold himself on what his job was all about. Then consider how many people there are in your territory who need what you sell, who are using obsolete equipment or inefficient methods that are costing them time, dollars, waste, customer satisfaction, frustration, you name it. Your job is to find those people and show them a better way.

The world is full of organizations vitally interested in ideas that will help them to function more effectively, assure their survival, help them keep pace with the rapidly changing times, increase productivity, make more profit, cut costs, improve morale, improve internal communications, reduce accidents, avoid legal problems, satisfy customers, avoid losing key employees, avoid wasted effort. Individuals are vitally interested in ways to gain recognition; make more effective use of time; get more enjoyment out of life; improve their financial situation; and to avoid mistakes, criticism, ridicule, fear, illness, death, pain, worry, or any one or combination of an unlimited number of concerns that are begging, sometimes silently, for solution.

To be sure, these concerns provide unlimited potential opportunities for salespeople all over the world. But before a transition can be made from potential to real opportunity, one must first become a provider of solutions.

And here we begin to answer the question, "Why should prospects let us into their world?"

First of all, as suggested in Chapter 2, they will when we are perceived as competent, knowledgeable experts in our field—well supplied with ideas, vital information, and other people's experience we can share.

Secondly, they will want to let us into their world when we put away our own personal concerns, forget what's in it for us when we make a call, and concentrate on what's in it for them—when we look out the window and see the people in the marketplace instead of looking in the mirror and seeing ourselves.

Prospects or Opponents?

A mistaken impression persists among people today that a top-notch salesperson is a suave, dynamic persuader like the mythical one who could sell refrigerators to Eskimos. Along with this myth, the notion persists that unless you're born with a superdynamic magnetism, you're never going to make it to the top in selling. Now that may have been true years ago in some less informed, less sophisticated era. But it certainly isn't true today. People are constantly being bombarded with sales pitches on television and through other media. Today, they are more knowledgeable, more alert, more sophisticated, more wary. What happens when you're approached by a suave, dynamic persuader? How do you feel? You're ready to lock the safe and hide the checkbook; all kinds of defenses and smokescreens go up.

Then there is a fallacy that persists among some salespeople who see selling as a contest. If a sale is made, the salesperson wins and the customer loses. The language of selling often sounds like a strategy for a boxing match. To make points in a presentation is to "hit 'em with this." Dialog with the prospect is called sparring. Response to resistance is commonly called overcoming objections and closing a sale is often referred to as delivering the knockout punch.

Hotshot Charlie Gets Burned

Let's follow a computer sales rep we'll call Charlie Smith on a call to Joe Johnson, president of the Gopher Company. On the way over to the appointment, Charlie chuckles to himself as he plans his approach: "Mr. Johnson ought to be a pushover. He'd probably go-fer anything, ha ha! I'll hit him with our new model 101. I'll make his eyes pop out when I show him the revolutionary super X feature. Then he'll knuckle under when he sees the complete software package. And I'll save our special finance plan for the coup de grace.''

One thing about Charlie, he is positive. Another thing, he is enthusiastic. That's all fine, but the problem is with the third thing—he is ready to do battle. The adrenaline is pumping in the same way it was when Charlie played left tackle in college and there was an enemy on the other side of the scrimmage line. If the third thing isn't enough to be Charlie's undoing, then the fourth is. Charlie is already planning how he's going to spend his commission check on this sale. Besides, this sale will put him in a special bonus bracket and that will make him enough money to afford the trip to Hawaii next January that he's been dreaming about. Just by coincidence, Charlie's car radio is playing Hawaiian music as he pulls into the Gopher Company parking lot.

Charlie greets Joe Johnson with a big smile and a hearty handshake, but Joe also sees the dollar signs in Charlie's eyes. Charlie is putting on an act for his own benefit, not Joe's, and Joe knows it. The coup de grace falls on Charlie when he wins an argument in logic, but loses the opportunity to make a sale.

Selling is not a contest. It is not a situation where one party wins and the other loses. Both can win. A prospect isn't someone to be tricked, manipulated, or dazzled with a phony act.

Prospects just don't want to be hit with unanswerable logic. They don't want to participate in a sparring match, much less be overcome and finally knocked out. People are like mirrors. They will reflect back to you your feelings toward them. If you see them as an enemy to be conquered, they will respond as the enemy putting up a defense, and their defensive position is a strong one. If you see them as a friend, they will return the friendship.

It's Easier to Be for Real

What is meant by reflecting feelings is much more than any external appearance or physical demeanor such as a friendly smile or a warm handshake. Smiles and handshakes are important! The friendlier and warmer, the better. But the underlying, deep-down, genuine feeling of warmth and friendliness must be there in order for the outward appearances to ring true. People today are more adept than ever before at detecting pretenders. They sense the tension between what is actually going on inside you and any mask you may choose to wear. You establish rapport when prospects believe you have an honest concern for their welfare and that you understand them.

It is true, as Harvard psychologist William James declared around the turn of the century, that feeling follows action. That is, if you act a certain way, the feeling that goes with that action will come over you, as in the familiar platitude, "To be enthusiastic, act enthusiastic."

The exception to William James's dictum is commonly found in pretense. A parallel has often been drawn between selling and acting, even by champions of the sales profession. The salesperson is "on stage," face to face with a prospect and "acting out" the presentation. This kind of dramatics can be effective in a selling situation only if the play being acted out is in complete harmony with the real feelings going on inside the actor/salesperson. Otherwise it is a turnoff.

In his book *The Mature Mind,* Harry Overstreet defines maturity as growing out of the self-contained ego—growing out of being self-centered and growing into becoming other-centered. We must not be very mature by Harry Overstreet's definition because psychologists tell us that we spend 85 percent of our time thinking about ourselves, about our own problems. Just stop and compare your untiring interest in what is happening in your own private world with your lack of concern about what is going on in the private world of almost everybody else. Realize that nearly everyone else alive is doing the same.

Your World and Theirs

Suppose you are about to call on Karen Weaver, a high-level executive in her company. Karen is busy. She is always busy. There is never enough time for her to do everything she feels she ought to do—deadlines to meet, meetings to attend, an in-basket that is never empty, constant interruptions from customers, her own staff, and yes, salespeople, many who turn out to be time wasters. Obviously Karen's mind is at least 95 percent occupied with her immediate concerns.

You just came out of a sales meeting. Your sales manager went on and on about the great company you represent, about all the wonderful services and products you have to offer, about the fantastic bells and whistles. You are also reminded about your sales quota for the month and how you need to go out there and make those calls to meet it. You are eager, excited, motivated!

As you approach Karen Weaver, you must do something unnatural. I say unnatural because the most natural thing for you to be thinking about is, "How am I going to tell Ms. Weaver about our great company, wonderful products, fantastic bells and whistles? I'll be on target to make my quota if I can do that."

And Ms. Weaver couldn't care less about all of that at this moment. To be invited into her world, you must first mentally get out of yours.

Chapter 3 dealt with the importance of a salesperson setting goals, especially to get new business. But goals tend to be selfish. Your goals express what you want to achieve. Prospects have a different set of goals. For sure, they don't care much about yours. This is especially true when you are a total stranger.

What do you think of this as an opening remark from a salesperson on a call? "Mr. Prospect, my company is in business to make a profit, and if you buy some of our products, it will help us to reach our profit objectives for this year."

Ridiculous, isn't it? You would never say that. But often salespeople say something like that nonverbally with their manner, with an outward expression of an inner concern. Communications experts have been telling us for years that the overwhelming effect of communication is nonverbal. It's not the words but the feelings that are being transmitted. Ralph Waldo Emerson put it eloquently when he said, "What you are stands over you . . . and thunders so that I cannot hear what you say to the contrary."

To say this is not to diminish the importance of goal setting. In selling, goals must be confined to the planning stages, which include writing call objectives. But when you are in contact with prospects, their goals take number one priority. The only way you can satisfy your goals is to satisfy theirs.

The Three Principles of Sales Psychology

The two principles of sales psychology we'll discuss first are:

1. People do things for their reasons, not yours.
2. Prospects are not much interested in your products or services. They are interested only in what your products or services will *do* for them.

How Do These Come Into Play?

Jean Miller bought a new sewing machine. Her husband, Todd, bought a set of deadbolt locks for the exterior doors of their home.

Pat O'Neill, vice president for sales for an insurance company, spent $20,000 for a sales incentive program.

Chester Kramer, resident of Pleasant Valley, bought a bag of the most expensive grass seed from his local garden store.

The Miller house is getting cluttered now that their four children are all teenagers. Jean really didn't want a sewing machine. It's just one more item to find room for. But the cost of buying ready-to-wear clothes for a family of six is more than the Millers' budget can stand. Besides, Jean really enjoys sewing. She bought cost reduction and pleasure.

Todd Miller didn't want any deadbolt locks. They are a bother to install and operate. But there have been several burglaries in the neighborhood recently. Todd bought security.

It was a struggle for Pat O'Neill to get budget approval for the incentive program. Several people on the executive committee didn't feel the company should be a Santa Claus to the agency force. Pat finally convinced them that profits from an expected sales increase would justify the expense.

No one, Chester Kramer included, wants seeds. Well, maybe birds do but they are not persons. Chester wants to have the greenest, thickest lawn on his block. He just loves to listen to compliments and he gets plenty regarding his beautiful lawn.

On my desk is a case for my eyeglasses. It has a clip that fastens to my inside coat pocket. I don't give a darn about that clip except for what it does for me. And do you know what that little clip does for me? Clipped to my inside coat pocket, the case just plain feels better there. It feels better clipped securely to the pocket instead of bouncing around loose at the bottom. Another thing I like about the clip is that when the case is clamped to my inside pocket it looks better, keeps the coat looking neat instead of showing a big lump. Feels better, looks better. That's what I like about the clip. Another thing, I'm less likely to lose my glasses. With the high cost of eyeglasses, that's going to save me some money. One more thing about the clip: I once took my coat off in the men's room and guess where the eyeglasses fell. You probably guessed right.

The eyeglass case is made out of genuine leather. Now I don't give a darn about that except for what it does for me. And do you know what it does for me? I once had an inexpensive plastic case. After a few months' use it was so dog-eared, I was embarrassed every time I took it out. The leather one has been in use for years. It looks just as good as new. It doesn't embarrass me.

You can talk about clips. Talk about what they are made of, about the finest imported spring steel. But all that doesn't mean a thing to me until I understand that clipping my eyeglass case to my pocket feels better, looks better, saves me money, and keeps my glasses from falling someplace where they could get messy. You could tick off all the great things about leather and that doesn't mean a thing unless I know that I won't be embarrassed by it and that it's going to save me money in the long run because it's not going to wear out.

The clip and the fact that the case is leather are features. Feel better, look better, save money, avoid embarrassment, avoid a mess are *benefits*.

And so we come to the third principle:

3. Benefits refer to people, not to products. Benefits refer to all the human satisfactions a person will enjoy from using the product. Any details that describe the product usually are not benefits.

Features, facts, and specifics are going to be of little interest to a buyer until the benefits are clearly in mind. The features simply prove that the benefits do in fact exist.

Just like my eyeglass case. I don't care about the clip, or how it's made, or what it's made of until I'm aware of the human satisfactions I will get from those features.

You may be thinking, "But I don't sell a product. I sell an intangible service."

It doesn't matter. In the third basic principle, substitute the word *service*—or whatever it is you call what you sell—for the word *product* and it will mean the same thing.

The place where it makes a difference whether you sell a product or a service is in a presentation. You can physically demonstrate a product.

For now, we are not talking about making presentations. We are talking about what we have to do or say at the initial contact point of a cold call to gain entry into the prospect's world. We are trying to make an appointment for a time to have a dialog with the prospect, which may involve a presentation or demonstration. We are talking about making an opening statement. Opening statements rarely include demonstrations.

Over the years I've heard many rhetorical discussions about the difference between selling tangibles and selling intangibles.

It is true that tangible products can be directly perceived by the senses—you can usually see them or see pictures of them, often touch them, perhaps even hear, taste, or smell them. But the sensory perceptions themselves are intangible, just as the reasons why people buy things are intangible.

Tangible products must ultimately be translated into benefits that satisfy intangible buying motives. To this extent all selling, whether of tangible products or intangible services, is much the same.

Benefits Defined

Behavioral scientists give us a profound insight that makes it easier for us to classify buying motives and translate them into benefits. It is this: *All human behavior can be traced to a person's desire for a feeling of well-being.* If people don't have a feeling of well-being, they want to find it. Or if they have a little of it, they want to increase it. If they already have the feeling of well-being, they want to avoid losing it. Or they want to avoid the opposite depressed feeling. Associated with these feelings of well-being are four primary motives that are the reasons behind almost everything that has ever been bought.

The first of these is *pride*. People want to gain or increase their feeling of pride. They want to own, use, and do things that will enhance their reputation and position. When you build a picture in a buyer's mind that offers recognition, approval, admiration, status, esteem, and ego satisfaction, you are selling benefits. Of course, you probably wouldn't use the words pride or ego satisfaction in your dialog. People don't like to admit those are important to them. You build a picture in their minds when you talk about an end result that they can identify in their world.

Suppose you were selling the grass seed to Chester Kramer. You might talk about another customer who bought that seed from you last year and how pleased he was when all of his neighbors raved about it.

On the other hand, people want to avoid criticism, ridicule, and disapproval. Consider how often you hear the expression, "What will the neighbors think?" That is fear of criticism. Or, "People must have thought I was nuts." That is fear of ridicule. These are powerful motives. Many people go through life with no more purpose than to get by with the least amount of discredit. They figure they've had a pretty good day at work if they don't catch heck from their boss.

There are countless examples of how powerful the pride motive is. When you explore the underlying causes of war, of threats of wars and consequent arms races, of suicides, of betrayed friendships, of marriage failures and broken homes, of mental breakdown, of personal conflict, even of vengeful murder, pride is high on the list.

Motive number two is that people want to increase their feelings of *pleasure,* and avoid the opposite feeling of pain or discomfort. They will pay readily and well for things and services that make them more comfortable, that make their lives and their work easier, that free them from mental and physical discomfort or drudgery. You are talking about benefits when you show people how their lives can be more fun, more exciting, or more interesting, or how you can help them do their jobs easier, faster, or better.

If you sell something that is similar to what a competitor sells, and your price is similar, then what must be the outstanding variable? You must be the variable. You must be a pleasure to do business with. You must offer a willingness to be of service, to provide counsel, guidance, or expertise that a competitor is unable or unwilling to provide. You are added value.

Motive number three is that people want to buy things that will help them either increase *profit* or avoid losses. This is a big one. More professional selling is aimed at this motive than any other. If you sell at the wholesale level, always keep in mind the fact that retailers don't want to stock their shelves

with a lot of merchandise; they just want to make a profit.
They want to hear the cash registers buzz. Whenever your
prospects are in business, it is important to make them feel
that your major purpose in life is to help them make more
profit or cut costs, or to help them get, hold, and satisfy
customers.

The fourth motive is that people want to buy what will
increase their feeling of *security* or what will help them avoid
anything that causes fear or anxiety. This covers things like
safety, peace of mind, health, and self-preservation. Companies maintain purchasing departments to buy all kinds of
goods and services to keep their business secure. Under
security motives, buyers often have unspoken questions on
their minds, such as: "Is it safe to buy from this person?" or
"How can I be sure what I hear is true?" Put yourself in the
buyer's place. Think of all the fears he may have and how you
can help him to avoid those fears.

For a quick look at these motives here they are in a matrix:

Gain	*Avoid*
Pride	Criticism or ridicule
Pleasure	Pain
Profit	Loss
Security	Fear or anxiety

You may have seen longer lists of motives. For example,
how about food, clothing, and shelter? Ordinarily, these needs
would be considered under security. But in our society today,
food is more often bought for the pleasure it gives. Clothing
is bought for pride. Shelter can be purchased for any one or
more of the four basic motives. Likewise, a person may gain
a great deal of pleasure from making a profit and that also
satisfies pride and security needs. So motives can be overlap-
ping. Sex attraction is a powerful force related to all four
motives. Profit? Why yes, the cosmetics industry does pretty
well appealing to that motive. Did you ever see anyone in a

cosmetics ad in a magazine or on TV who didn't look prosperous?

The Essence of Selling

It doesn't matter that the product you sell or your business may be different from that of other salespeople. The people that you sell to are pretty much the same with the basic human needs, wanting the same basic benefits. Virtually every human being you come into contact with will be stimulated into buying, or even just listening to your presentation, by these same basic motives. Truly these represent the real reason why almost any purchase is ever made.

For example, I sell intangibles—sales training programs, seminars, consulting services, and program design. I also sell tangibles such as books, manuals, films, and audio and video cassette programs. Those words describe what it is I sell. But clients buy increased sales and profits, more new accounts, reduced sales costs, reduced turnover and raised morale of a sales force, more effective use of salespersons' time, increased market share, upgraded clientele, and sales managers' time saved in preparation of sales meetings.

So then, what you sell in your product or service is not its features, or its function, or its price, or its quality, or its size or volume or shape or color. Selling, in its purest sense, is simply translating all that factual information into the benefits that serve the prospect's self-interest whether it be pride, pleasure, profit, or security. That is not to say you must use all four of those appeals every time. Often just one is the most important concern of a particular prospect. In that case you need only concentrate on that one. For example, if you sell to business firms, you can be pretty sure they want to make more profit or cut costs. If you're not sure what the main buying motive is, a few timely questions can help you avoid making wrong assumptions. In Chapter 8 you will learn how to determine a prospect's dominant buying motive by using effective probing techniques. One wrong assumption you want to avoid, however, is that the people you approach will make the translation from product features to human satisfactions themselves.

Experienced Salespeople Please Take Heed

If you are an experienced, trained salesperson these last few pages may not have covered anything particularly new to you. But I urge you not to shrug it off as old hat too quickly.

As a consultant, I often make calls with my clients' salespeople. I may be doing a needs analysis, coaching, or trouble shooting. On a needs analysis clients most often assign their most experienced people to me. This gives me a quickest overview of their selling situation. It never ceases to amaze me how often I work with experienced professionals who know the basics of selling but fail to apply them.

"Knowledge is power" a wise sage said centuries ago. Ever since, we have been repeating that phrase presuming it was absolute. A more recent sage said, "The world is full of educated derelicts." This suggests that power lies in the application of knowledge, not in the knowledge itself.

"Knowing" the basics of effective selling is relatively easy to learn. Applying them is more difficult because it goes against our natural inclination.

It is natural for us to be thinking about *what it is* we are selling.

It is not natural for us to be thinking from the prospect's point of view, which is, *what will it do for me?*

Prospects are thinking, "Don't tell me how good your goods are until you tell me how good your goods are going to make me."

Therefore you must make a deliberate, conscious, extraordinary effort to disengage your mind from your world. Especially resist the natural impulse to begin a sales call by bragging about what it is you are selling. That is exactly what prospects expect you to do. You are then sounding like every other salesperson who called recently. Many of them were time wasters. Therefore you are likely to be categorized as a time waster also. The prospect's natural impulse is to get rid of you as quickly as possible.

Avoid a Fatal Assumption

Jerry Clement's point of view is typical of many salespeople I've met. Jerry was on the sales staff of a chemical manufacturer client of mine. I was assigned to spend a day working with him as part of a training needs analysis I was preparing for the company. When making calls with salespeople during a needs analysis, I never coach or critique their performance. My task is strictly to ask questions and observe.

Jerry knew his products well. He prided himself on the fact that he could quote facts verbatim from the brochures and catalog sheets. Inasmuch as he knew I was in the sales training business, Jerry wanted to express his opinion of the company's past efforts in that department. "Last year at the annual sales meeting," Jerry recalled, "we spent three days role-playing on explaining the benefits in the features of our products. You know, that all sounds good in theory but we can't really use that stuff on a call. Most of the people we call on have degrees in chemistry. They know what our products do. I'd feel foolish if I had to say all of those obvious things."

Now Jerry may be right in assuming that many of the people he calls on know what his products do. But Jerry is wrong if he assumes they will be thinking of those benefits when he comes to call.

Because benefits are not inherent in the product or service being sold. Benefits are in the prospect's mind. If they are not in the prospect's mind at the moment you approach, you must put them there or they will not exist for the prospect at that particular moment! Features can exist without the prospect, but the benefits cannot.

Be mindful of this especially when making first-time calls on new prospects. If they are preoccupied with other matters, if they are wondering whether or not you are a time waster, if they are thinking they're satisfied with their present situation, or any one of numerous other ifs, it's a pretty safe assumption the benefits will not be in their minds unless you make a special effort to help them focus on benefits.

Whatever else you may concern yourself with on a call, there is one omnipresent reality you must deal with. That reality is in the mind of the prospect. You must *position* yourself favorably in that reality. Nothing else matters as much. On a cold call you must secure a favorable position in the prospect's mind as quickly as possible. Then you become a higher priority in his or her day. Consider how you prioritize your tasks on an ongoing basis (as every good salesperson should). Prospects do the same. Positioning is establishing a place on this ongoing, ever-changing priority list.

Never take for granted that the benefits are self-evident. The essence of the task of selling is to translate product features into benefits *in the mind* of the prospective buyer. In becoming properly familiar with a product, it is easy to lose sight of the fact that buyers just don't have the initial interest to spend time and effort making the translation for themselves. They may know what the benefits are, but if they are not thinking benefits, your efforts will be for naught. Even a low price by itself doesn't mean much. Only when a person is aware that the sum total of benefits is going to equal or exceed the price will that person be willing to pay the price. Likewise, only when a person is aware that the benefits of listening to your presentation are going to equal or exceed the value of the time spent will that person be willing to spend the time.

Simplify Your Approach

Perhaps in previous sales training you learned of an inter-mediate element between a feature and a benefit known as an *advantage*. The idea here is you first convert a feature into an advantage before it is translated into a benefit. An advantage is usually defined as the way a feature is used to solve a problem. For example, if you were selling some kind of machine, you might say, "This machine has sealed bearings [feature], so it will never require oiling [advantage], and that will make your job easier [benefit].'' I find this extra step causes confusion in the minds of many salespeople. I've listened to many useless discussions about whether something is an advantage or a benefit. The fine line between an advantage and a benefit is often blurred. There may be more reason to consider an advantage as an extra step in a detailed or technical presentation that allows time to make demonstrations that include advantages. But an introductory remark aimed at gaining the attention of a prospect needs to be shorter.

Better to keep it simple. Better to just keep clear in your mind the basic principle that people do things for their reasons, not yours. Better to spend your time and effort in discovering what those reasons are. Better to be thinking of ways to translate the features of what you sell into a combination of advantages and benefits to your prospects without mentally struggling with which is an advantage and which is a benefit. Whether advantages or benefits, both are in the buyer's interest.

Offer Plus Values

In addition to benefits directly related to features of your product, give some thought to possible benefits unrelated to the product itself. These could be any service you have to offer, such as technical assistance, merchandising, co-op advertising, resale help, billing, financing, market research, delivery, or any other service that is unique to your business. Of course, also keep in mind the counsel, guidance, and useful ideas you can offer on the basis of your experience and know-how.

One of my clients is a mobile-home manufacturer. A problem its dealer organization faces, especially when interest rates are high, is financing the inventory on its sales lots. The manufacturer developed a superb audiovisual presentation that showed every model and every possible combination of interior design it makes. It even designed one of its models as a studio to show the presentation. The benefit to the dealer, unrelated to the product itself, was increased profits through opportunities to make more sales and at reduced inventory expense. Such extra benefits often will give you a competitive edge, especially when price competition may be a factor. Buyers become less concerned about price when benefits unrelated to the product itself offer plus values.

Keeping on Track

Here is an idea to help you assimilate the principles outlined in this chapter. It will also be useful to you in Chapter 6 when we will consider the composition of an effective opening statement.

At the top of sheet of paper write the question: "Why should a prospect listen to me?" Then write down as many different answers to that question as you can think of without mentioning or describing the product or service you sell. Answer the question in terms of benefits to your prospects and in terms of the human satisfaction they will realize just from granting you an interview. Remember, an important benefit is the information, ideas, and other people's experience you are in a position to share.

Then take several three-by-five-inch cards and with a marking pen write this question on each card in large, bold letters: "WHAT DO I REALLY SELL?" Now attach one card to the sun visor of your car, put another in a prominent position on your desk, another inside your briefcase, and another in any other place where you will notice it as you go about your day. Then several times a day, especially just before a call on a prospect either in person or on the phone, answer that question to yourself in as many ways as you can think of without mentioning or describing the product you sell. Answer that question in terms of benefits to your customers, in terms of all the human satisfactions they will enjoy as a result of dialog with you and doing business with you.

Before making a call, check your inner dialog. Ask yourself if you are going there to help someone solve a problem or to use someone to help solve yours. In your self-talk use positive, uplifting words to describe your role, such as problem finder, problem solver, consultant, idea giver, helper. Avoid words that suggest conflict—don't refer to your selling points as something to "hit 'em with," your precall planning as preparation for the attack, sales tools as weapons in your arsenal to overcome objections, and closing the sale as a victory.

As you continue your personal growth in becoming more confident, competent, and knowledgeable in your field, and as you perceive the importance of that kind of growth more deeply, the people you call on will recognize your competence also. There will be no need for pretense or phony dramatics. Nor will you be handicapped with unnecessary stress caused by the burden of maintaining a contrived or combative posture. You can relax and just be yourself and let that natural personality do the job for you. Selling will become easier, more enjoyable, and more productive.

You will put a lot more "sell" in your selling efforts when you consciously and deliberately think and talk about all the good things your product or service will do for prospects instead of what it is, about what's in it for them instead of what's in it for you, about benefits instead of features.

You will be more eager to make calls, as you will feel better about yourself and your job. You will no longer feel that prospects are doing you a favor by granting an audience, but rather that you are the one with favors to offer with profitable ideas, counsel, guidance, and professional expertise, in addition to the benefits to be gained from your product or service. For when your concern is truly for your prospects, your words will flow with a sincerity of purpose and natural enthusiasm that will be both captivating and convincing.

Chapter 6

PLANNING
THE OPENING MOVE

Often in my seminars, someone in the audience asks, "Is it better to phone for an appointment or make an in-person approach?" In my opinion that is not the question to ask. Questions to ask are: Under what conditions is it better to phone for an appointment? Under what conditions is it better to just walk in? How skilled are you in using the phone? To arrive at the best answer for you, compare the advantages of using a phone with the advantages of in-person calls.

Advantages of Opening on the Phone

- The greatest advantage of telephoning is the convenience and speed with which you can reach the largest numbers of potential prospects. If you can quickly separate prospects from suspects or can quickly evaluate the relative priority you will want to assign to prospects, the phone is your primary tool.

- You don't need to be all dressed up for business.
- You save the cost of gas and car maintenance, travel tickets, meals, and lodging on the road.
- You don't waste valuable selling time fighting traffic, traveling long stretches, waiting for public carriers, or sitting in reception lobbies.
- You can call anywhere in the world from anywhere else in the world at any time of the day.
- When buying patterns are seasonal or affected by sudden swings of market conditions, it may be impossible to cover your territory otherwise. Once, as I was conducting an all-day seminar at a flour milling company sales meeting, we had to interrupt it at 11:00 A.M. Everyone scattered to find telephones as a shock wave hit flour prices.
- You are not at the mercy of weather. And if you live in snow and ice country, you know what that means.
- You can take notes and use a script without the prospect knowing or being distracted by your action.
- When calling from your office, you have files and information at your fingertips.
- It is easier to get to the point on the phone without seeming abrupt.
- The prospect focuses attention on the matter at hand rather than on you. This is particularly helpful if you have any nervous mannerisms that can be distracting.
- Not always but often, people will drop what they are doing to answer the phone. They may not allow an interruption for an unknown, in-person visitor.

Advantages of In-Person Openers

- It is easier to terminate a phone conversation than it is to dismiss an in-person visitor. That is one reason why people are more willing to allow a phone call to interrupt their preoccupation.
- You can see the prospect's body language, which often bears important clues to what is actually happening.

- You have an opportunity to make observations of the prospect's physical property, the size of the operation, the names on doors. You can get information from employees, neighbors, and literature. Needs may be apparent that you can discern only by being there. Remember Fred Hawkins and the truckload of unfinished components in Chapter 2.
- You may have a personal appeal that comes across only in a face-to-face contact.
- There is an increasing trend toward telephone selling— even computer-actuated, recorded voices. Buyers, executives, and their staff assistants, as well as the public at large, are becoming more sensitive to and sophisticated in resisting telephone approaches.
- You may have striking visual material that would help to neutralize initial resistance.
- There will be many opportunities in person when you will get "slide in" or "spot" presentations. That is, you will go right from the opener to the interview to the presentation and at times make a sale all in one call. Some of those prospects on the phone would have easily brushed you off. Others would have postponed setting the appointment, requiring frustrating callbacks. Still others would have cooled off completely or bought from a competitor in the meantime.
- Making drop-in calls is sound time and territory management. When you are in a certain vicinity and have time between appointments, such calls are excellent fill-in use of time.
- Many salespeople are temperamentally unsuited to sit for any length of time at the phone. It takes a special kind of discipline to keep an enthusiastic momentum going. Inexperienced phone salespeople and those who don't like to do it will spend an inordinate amount of time shuffling prospect cards or resorting to other diversions. Discouragement comes quicker because turndowns come quicker. One must be prepared to deal with the special kind of stress that comes with extended telephone use.

- Unskilled phone salespeople often use ill-advised "cherry picking" methods. Cherry picking is classifying prospects into categories of cherries or pits. The cherries are those who offer little or no initial resistance. The pits are the difficult ones and are quickly dropped from the list. You may get by doing that if your field of prospective clients is unlimited and if each client is a one-time sale. But it doesn't make good sense if your market is specialized or if you have identified certain target prospects that offer great potential, especially if that potential involves repeat sales over many future years.

As you can see, whether or not to use the phone has no general right or wrong answer. For more on the use of the phone, see Chapter 14, "Sharpening Your Telephone Skills." That chapter will help you improve your telephone techniques. Be aware that, with the exception of Chapter 14, the principles in this book generally apply to both telephone sales and in-person visits.

Defining Some Terms

The readers of this book are probably involved in a variety of selling situations. While some few may make quick, one-call sales based on a brief presentation or demonstration, it is safe to assume that most will require enough dialog to warrant arranging an appointment for a convenient time for prospects to give the dialog the necessary attention. The dialog usually involves probing for needs, an interview and a presentation of some length, responding to resistance, and gaining commitment.

The presentation centers on proving you can satisfy the need, building desire and conviction, and closing the sale, or in the case of a more complex selling situation, setting up a subsequent phase. Some salespeople prefer to call their presentation an interview when it is more of a give-and-take verbal exchange rather than mostly monolog. Some make a distinction between an interview and a presentation. The interview part is further dialog to get a better understanding of the prospect's situation, whereas the presentation is directed toward relating benefits, explaining features, offering proof or a demonstration, or showing a line of merchandise. Actually, probing for needs is in itself an interview, and the line between probing and the interview can get blurred. Sometimes, at your suggestion, or at the prospect's invitation, your presentation will be given immediately following the opener or the probe. For all practical purposes that is an appointment. It just happened to be made on the spot.

I don't intend to cover such things as making presentations, closing sales, and resistance after an attempted close in great detail. I am concerned only with setting up presentations on the right basis and dealing with opening resistance.

As we get into specific techniques, not everything I suggest can be expected to apply absolutely 100 percent to every selling situation. Situations vary, people vary. There are always exceptions. I'm describing what I've discovered works best, most often, in most situations. People who are trained in math or sciences sometimes get uncomfortable with that. In science, you mix A with B under temperature C and pressure D and it always comes out exactly the same.

Selling is not like that. Selling is more of an art than a science. You may take exception to some of my suggestions. When you do, don't throw the baby out with the bathwater. Don't let the things that don't apply to you prevent you from using the things that do apply and from which you could profit.

Some more complex selling situations involve several phases of contact over a long period of time. It would be impossible to detail all the various types of possibilities. The main purpose in setting forth the following sequence is to define some terms we will use. Therefore, the sequence is given according to the most typical progression.

Here, then, is the sequence of events on a new contact up to the point of presentation:

The Opening Statement

This is sometimes called the opener and consists of three parts: an introduction of yourself and your company, an opening benefit, and a request for an appointment.

Remember, a cold call is always an interruption. You can be certain that prospects are not sitting around waiting for your call. Therefore you need to sell your prospects on continuing a dialog with you now or at a future time. You want them to suspect that they will be missing something very important if they don't let you into their world.

The purpose of an opener, then, is to introduce yourself and your company and to arrange for the interview and presentation to take place under the most advantageous circumstances. It is important to keep this primary objective clearly in mind and not to get ahead of it prematurely.

Did you ever see a receiver in football start advancing downfield before having full control of the ball? What usually happens? You're right, an incomplete pass or a fumble. Likewise in golf. Did you ever get caught looking ahead and muff a shot as a result? "Keep your eye on the ball" is a well-worn cliché. By some quirk of human nature, most of us have to make a disciplined effort to do that—to concentrate on one single step at a time.

The same holds true in the opening phase of a sale. Getting an appointment on the right basis is a sale in itself. It is critically important and requires intense concentration.

Openers may be compared to previews that advertise a movie. Their aim is to tantalize—to stir up enough interest and curiosity to make you want to come back and see the whole thing. If too much of the plot is disclosed, you might prejudge it in a way that would cool off motivation to come back. If it doesn't tell enough of what the movie is all about, that too will fail to arouse your desire to come back.

The same with a good opener. You need to guard against adverse prejudgment on the part of your prospects. Prejudgment is one of the biggest stumbling blocks you will encounter on a cold call. Tell them no more about your proposition than is necessary to arouse their interest and curiosity so that they will agree to arrange for the time necessary to learn all about it. It is usually a mistake to try to tell them all about it in the opener phase. Of course, there will be opportunities for "slide in" interviews and spot presentations. On a cold call, however, you would ordinarily ask the prospect if it is convenient for you to continue. So for practical purposes an appointment is being set. It just happened that it is set to immediately follow your opener. But until you do that, it is still the opening phase and your objective is only to set the appointment on the most favorable basis.

The Prospect Responds

The response is usually one or a combination of several of these:

1. *Interest.* The prospect admits to a need and agrees to an appointment.
2. *Indifference.* Prospects are indifferent when they don't see a need for what you sell. They are often complacent or satisfied with their present situation.
3. *Skepticism.* Skeptical prospects are likely to have a need and know it but do not believe everything said regarding your claimed ability to satisfy their need.
4. *Objections.* Prospects responding with objections during the opener also are likely to have a need and know it. But they also know, or prejudge, something about you, your company, or your product and make some negative remark.
5. *An indefinite appointment is made.* That is, the prospect declines to set a specific time for an appointment and asks you to phone at another time to confirm it.
6. *Complete lack of interest.* The prospect chooses to terminate the contact.

Probing for Needs

When the prospect resists your opening request for an appointment, you then ask questions to discover needs and important factual information, as well as the emotional background that will help you decide how to proceed. In my experience in making calls with salespeople, I find this is the juncture at which they fail most often in the sequence of dialog with a prospect on a cold call. They are not prepared to ask questions. They are too quick to give up at the first sign of resistance. They either hang up the phone or turn tail and exit on an in-person call. Probing for needs is the primary technique for dealing with indifference, skepticism, and objections. More about that later. Even when the response to the opener is affirmative, you may probe to qualify the prospect according to your criteria.

Offering a Benefit to Satisfy the Need

I often hear arguments about the difference between needs and wants. Some claim it's more important to sell to people's wants rather than needs. That may be true in selling something like a luxury automobile as opposed to the need for transportation. But for most practical purposes and certainly if you are selling to business firms or nonprofit institutions, the word *need* is more applicable.

Depending on the situation, *want, problem, dissatisfaction,* and *need* all have useful connotations. For the sake of simplicity, I use the word *need* to represent any of those four meanings except where the special connotation of another word will fit better. When at least one important need is identified, suggest a benefit that corresponds with the need.

Ask for an Appointment

It's important that you take the initiative to suggest a specific time for further dialog.

Spotlight the Benefit

Recall the three parts of an opener: introduction of yourself and your company, an opening benefit, and a request for an appointment.

The first part, the introduction of yourself and your company, requires no unusual creative effort. You've been doing it for years. It's best to use words that come easily and naturally to you.

Some sales managers train their reps to not even introduce themselves at first when making in-person calls, but rather to get right into the benefit. Their feeling is the rep's identity is of little importance compared with the benefit. Hence, don't say anything that will take the spotlight off the benefit.

Yes, the most important consideration is the opening benefit. It gives the prospect a reason for wanting to listen to you. It's a good idea to review Chapter 5 to get a better understanding of why certain words and phrases will be most effective. Remember that people do things for their reasons, not yours. They are not going to be interested in what you sell or the fact that you want to sell it. They will be interested only in what good it can do for them. And as you are saying your opening lines, their immediate interest is deciding whether or not talking to you any further would be of any benefit to them.

Avoid These Common, Weak Openers

In all my years of working with salespeople in the field training, coaching, and evaluating performance, one of the most common opening lines I hear after the introduction is ordinarily one of the weakest! "Could I have a few minutes of your time?"

What kind of benefit is that? For busy people, reaction to the thought of giving a few minutes of their time to a total stranger without good reason is bound to be negative. Besides, it sounds as if you lack confidence in yourself and what you are going to say. Thus it gives the prospect even more reason to give you a quick brush-off. Of course, you must check to find out when it is convenient for a prospect to visit at length. Just don't make that your opening line. It belongs in the request for an interview but not your very first utterance.

There are sales trainers who will tell you that the first thing you must do when on the phone is to "take the curse off the call." I ask you, who is putting the curse on the call? If you choose to identify your call as a curse, if it becomes a curse in your mind, then it is bound to become a curse in the mind of the prospect. Get rid of the notion that it is a curse. It is not. Remember, you are loaded with information and other people's experience that you are willing to share.

At times on an in-person call, you may find it necessary to interrupt someone you can see is busy. Even then, "May we talk for a few minutes?" is much better than "Could I have a few minutes of your time?"

Or when you go through a third party such as a receptionist or a secretary, chances are that the person you want to see is busy doing something else at that moment. You will then have to wait in the outer lobby until it is convenient for your prospect to see you. So when you get face to face, you are expected to say something. You don't need to ask permission for initial time. You will need to ask for time only when you continue beyond the opener.

Openers should be very brief. When you go beyond the opener, you are into an interview or a presentation. Before you get that far, make sure you're doing it with some indication of the prospect's compliance. To make sure of that, it's best to ask for time outright. But the time to ask for it is after you state a benefit, not in the opening line, unless it is an interruption. Other poor opening lines are:

- Sorry to bother you but . . .
- Is this a bad time?
- I'd like to get an appointment with you . . .
- I just happened to be in the neighborhood . . .
- I was wondering if you might be interested in . . .
- I wanted to visit with you for a few minutes about . . .
- I'd like to get your business . . .

Again, what benefits are expressed or implied in those statements? Obviously none. To make a call just because you're in the neighborhood is to apologize for it. Busy people don't care much what strangers are wondering or what they want. Be sure to take those I-oriented statements out of your opener. You don't want to give the impression that you want an appointment for your reasons. Remember to talk only about their reasons, not yours.

In the business world, persons with the right buying authority to whom you want to state your opener are not to be found in the outer lobby on an in-person call. Nor are they the ones who ordinarily answer the telephone. Your first contact is usually a receptionist. Then you often are greeted by a secretary or administrative assistant before you have an opportunity to state your opener to your intended prospect. In Chapter 12, I cover dialog with such gatekeepers, but at this point we will assume you have gone beyond the gatekeepers and are speaking directly to your intended prospect.

Composing Opening Statements

I don't want to put words in your mouth. Rather, let me suggest some ingredients that have proven to be effective in an opening statement. These ingredients are a distillation of many years, working with many different clients selling a wide variety of products and services, and through trial and error, discovering what works best. It's important that you learn the ingredients. But it is even more important that you learn why the ingredients are suggested. Then you will be better able to select words that are uniquely your own.

The first of these ingredients is the prospect's name. There is no sweeter music to the ears of most people than the sound of their own name. Use it! We are conditioned to be alert and listen when we hear our name.

You will meet prospects whose names are difficult to pronounce. Be sure you pronounce them correctly. Don't be shy about asking for the correct pronunciation. You are not going to offend anyone by asking. On your prospect card write out the phonetic pronunciation so you will get it right on subsequent calls. It's a safe bet that most other salespeople calling on that person will not take the time and trouble to get it right, and your prospect will be pleased with your diligence. This is one more way to gain an edge over competition.

The question is often asked: "Is it better to use the first name or the last name?" There are some people who are offended by strangers, especially sales types, who get too familiar too soon in a relationship. On the other hand there are some who prefer to be called by first name. So how do you know the difference?

On a phone call if someone answers by saying, "Chuck here," it's a safe bet you have someone who doesn't mind being called by his first name. But unless you have some indication of first-name preference, better to play it safe and use the last name. Why risk offending someone who would take exception to overfamiliarity? Especially someone who could eventually turn out to be one of your best customers. But that will never come to pass if you blow it on the first contact. Obviously use Mr. for a man; women give us a choice.

A perplexing question for sales reps is, "How do you greet the feminist-era woman?" Some women still don't like the title Ms. prefixed to their name and probably never will. So when you hear a name like Betty Ross, what do you call her?

A "by the way" parting question to the receptionist can clear it up. When you are faced with a woman and don't know her preference, the advice I get from a consensus of women I polled is to use Ms. If she has a strong preference for Miss or Mrs., she will usually correct you and that's that. Whatever you do, don't make a big deal out of it.

Using Ms. as a prefix to a last name is certainly preferable to opting to use the first name with a total stranger in a business situation. The exception is when someone introduces herself with a first name only.

In the prefeminist days, men were to wait until a woman initiated a handshake. Now either sex can be first to extend a hand in greeting.

Another ingredient is the call objective. Announce the fact

that you have a call objective with words something like this:
"Ms. Prospect, my special reason for calling on you today
is . . ." If you don't like to use the word "special," omit it.
But I prefer to use it. I want that prospect to know that I'm
not "just in the neighborhood," nor am I sitting in a boiler
room making one random phone call after another. I've done
some homework. I've done some thinking about that prospect's particular situation. I have, in fact, come up with a
special reason for the call. If you can say the word "special"
with honesty and conviction, you will sound entirely different
from most other salespeople who call.

Here are two more reasons why I like to use this phrase.
First, it forces me to have a call objective. I could not evade
it. Second, it forces me to be thinking of that call objective at
that particular moment. I could not avoid it.

An Especially Powerful Word

The next ingredient is an extremely versatile and powerful
four-letter word—a clean four-letter word—that works won-
ders in virtually any opener. Of the many different products
all of my clients or I personally have been involved in selling,
I have never known of a product or service for which it does
not apply. It in fact replaces the word that stands for any
service or product. It is that universal. Its very use automatically implies a benefit!

The word is *idea*.

No matter what you sell, there must be some ideas connected with how it is used, or purchased, or financed, or sold,
or something. Somewhere from your experience with other
customers, or from reports that you heard from others in your
company, or from an article in a trade magazine, you must
know of a unique or especially creative use of your product
that can become a special idea—an idea that provides a
benefit. It's an idea that will make the prospect more money,
cut costs, or do a job more easily, faster, or whatever.

At the moment you introduce yourself, a prospect may not
even be remotely interested in what you sell. But the prospect

will likely be interested in considering an idea that will offer a solution to a problem, or provide some special benefit. Ideas are such powerful things. All the marvels of our space age, all of our modern conveniences, today's medical miracles, all creation for that matter, first were ideas.

Socrates said, "Small minds discuss people. Average minds discuss events. But great minds discuss ideas!"

Every day hundreds of thousands of people pay a substantial registration fee to attend seminars. Some have to fly to another city and stay in expensive hotels. If they are revenue-producing personnel, the dollars of revenue lost by sitting in seminars often far exceeds the cost of seminar registration, airfare, meals, and lodging. Yet they are willing, or their company is willing, to pay the price. Why? To get some ideas that will help them to become more effective on their jobs. This is proof that people are hungry for ideas. They are willing to pay a substantial price for ideas. Here you come along and are offering them free of charge.

But don't be like the sales rep who opened with, "Mr. Prospect, I have an idea that can make you a whole lot of money."

The prospect motioned toward a chair saying, "Come in and sit down. I'm always willing to listen to ideas like that. What's your idea?"

"Well, I really don't have one, but wasn't that a heck of an opener?" the wag replied.

Be sure you have a solid idea, well planned, backed up with proof that relates to a prospect's self-interest.

If I haven't given you enough reasons to use the word *idea,* let me give you several more. The word *idea* arouses curiosity. Stimulating curiosity has a powerful force of attraction. Remember the grab bags in the candy store? They always sold well. Kids couldn't resist finding out what was inside.

Using the word *idea* forces you to do something I said in Chapter 5 that is critically important. It forces you to take your mind off what it *is* you are selling and center it on to what it will *do* for the prospect, because the idea has to do with an intangible benefit.

Using the word *idea* prevents prejudgment. Remember, prejudgment is one of the biggest stumbling blocks on a cold call. The minute you name what it is you are selling, prospects will compare it with something they are familiar with and often quickly decide they are not going to be interested.

You may recall the benefit statement I use when selling my sales training services: ". . . an idea that my clients tell me helps their salespeople to generate more new business."

Sales training isn't mentioned. I don't want the prospect to mentally compare my program with something they may have experienced in the past that has nothing to do with mine and may have been unsatisfactory.

At this point it could be something besides sales training. For instance, it could be a sales incentive program, or a door opening gimmick, or an audiovisual presentation device, or a lot of other things. Often the prospect's curiosity is aroused sufficiently to want to know more about it. But that will be revealed only on my terms, which are an appointment for an interview and a presentation made under circumstances most favorable for me to understand the prospect's situation, and for the prospect to understand how my program can be of benefit.

If you sell insurance, they don't want to buy more insurance. Stocks, banking services, printing, office equipment, packaging, or whatever you are selling—they probably are already well taken care of.

Busy people don't want you to add to the confusion they are already experiencing by interrupting what they are doing to consider another source. Even if they are not completely satisfied with their present source, at least they have grown accustomed to it and have been getting by. You are an unknown, therefore a risk.

Besides, what you sell obviously is going to cost them money. And if you're talking about the bells and whistles, they are going to cost even more. But ah! The idea. That is free.

Of course, you can have more than one idea and say so by using the plural, *ideas*.

Bring in the Witnesses

Immediately following the word *idea* another potent and convincing phrase is, "Our customers tell us," or, "Our customers find." Instead of *customers* you may prefer the word *clients,* or there may be special terminology in your industry. For example, in the trucking business customers are called *shippers.* In the seed industry it is *growers.*

In an opener, you must establish credibility early and quickly. This magic phrase packs a considerable amount of believability into your benefit statement. A prospect would rightly expect you to make positive claims about your product. But now it isn't you making the claim. You're like a reporter relating a claim made by a neutral third party who doesn't have any self-serving motive in helping you to reach your objective. A buyer would have to admit to a measure of stubbornness if such an endorsement were totally ignored.

The Benefit Is Revealed

Now you are ready to reveal the benefit. Go back to page 80 where it was suggested that you write out an answer to the question, "Why should a prospect listen to me?" If you haven't taken the time to answer that question yet, do it now. Do some creative brainstorming to write as many answers to that question as you can think of. When possible do this with other salespeople in your company. Two or more minds make a strong creative force. Remember the rules of brainstorming—go after a large quantity of ideas. No criticism or negative comments are allowed during the idea-generating time. Do your judging and refining later. Compose your answers in such a way as to paint word pictures of benefits—the more specific to the prospect's world, the better. Show how you can help them to function more effectively; assure their survival; help them keep pace with the rapidly changing times; increase productivity; make more profit; cut costs; improve morale and internal communications; reduce accidents, downtime, and rejects; attract, satisfy, and keep customers; avoid mistakes, wasted effort, legal problems, or losing key employees; make more effective use of time; get more enjoyment out of work and life; avoid criticism, ridicule, fear, illness, death, pain, worry, or embarrassment; or profit from any special benefits your product offers.

These are all general benefits. Now translate them or attach them to something specific in the prospect's world.

Joining the Ingredients

Now you have a simple formula to showcase an interest-catching, opening benefit:

1. The prospect's name
2. A special reason for the call
3. An idea
4. Our customers tell us
5. Provides a specific benefit

A complete opening benefit would go something like this:

> Mr. Washington, my special reason for calling on you today is to show you an idea that our customers tell us reduces hours of labor by at least 20 percent on the assembly of gear boxes similar to the one on your model 102.

This is an example of a specific benefit. You would have done some homework in order to refer to something specific in the prospect's world. You learned that a component of his production is a gear box on a model 102. You also must have learned something about how it was assembled. Such specific benefits are definitely preferable if you have access to that kind of information.

When you don't know the specific details of a prospect's possible needs, you would give a less specific benefit with the expectation of doing some probing to uncover a specific need in the interview phase. Your opener would then go like this:

Mr. Washington, my special reason for calling on you today is to show you an idea that our customers tell us reduces hours of labor by as much as 20 percent in some manufacturing processes.

Other examples are:

- An idea that our customers tell us . . .
- . . . increased profits by creating a whole new market for your kind of products.
- . . . produced significant cost reductions by reducing rejects from employee carelessness.
- . . . increased customer satisfaction by helping them find the best source of supply to fit each customer's particular needs.
- . . . greatly reduced operating costs while at the same time upgraded their positioning in the marketplace.
- . . . solved problems of healthcare cost containment, cost protection, and cost documentation.
- . . . increased profit by generating more profit per unit sold.
- . . . reduced operating costs and at the same time enhanced employee relations.

It is not necessary to link a feature of your product or service to the benefit you are leading with in your opener. Talking about features, proving why benefits happen, belongs in the presentation, not in the opener. Putting features in your opener is going too far, too fast, making it more complicated, harder for the prospect to follow, and risking prejudgment. Your best opener will hold a spotlight on the benefit—the end result. The only time to talk about a feature in the opener is when the feature is something extraordinary that would arouse curiosity or for some other reason would merit sharing the spotlight with the benefit.

Stay away from threadbare clichés such as, "This is the best buy," "We are the greatest," "We are the fastest growing," or "Acclaimed the world over." Such meaningless superlatives suggest that anything else you say is going to be meaningless and overstated.

Details in your situation may vary from those presumed in the above example. That may require some alternative phrasing. For example, you may have a brand-new product that does not yet have a customer track record. Then instead of quoting a satisfied customer, get an opinion of a prominent authority in your field. Or say, "That has been tested and proved to . . . [solve a particular problem that is common to your clientele]."

In many instances you will have a pretty good idea of the prospect's needs. Your product is designed and being sold to meet some kind of need; otherwise it wouldn't exist. You're calling on people facing similar problems. Making more profit is universal in business. Cutting costs has an even wider range of need. Also, there is no reason why you can't mention two or three benefits in an opening statement.

When Your Benefit Misfires

Occasionally the benefit you lead with will be off target. For example, supposing Mr. Washington were planning to phase out his model 102, or it were being redesigned without a gear box. And you didn't know that. Then quickly switch to a general benefit. At least you are a lot closer to his interest than if you had "just happened to be in the neighborhood."

Qualifying Prospects

A common situation is that you may not be sure your suspect is a prospect. Or you may sell a wide variety of products or services that have many different applications. In advance of a call, you have no information as to how your idea could fit into a prospect's situation. Therefore, you will need additional dialog to probe for needs. Take this approach:

Mr. Lincoln, my company is serving many manufacturers with an idea that our customers find substantially reduces hours of labor on certain manufacturing processes. My special purpose in calling on you today is to find out if it would have an application to your business. Could I get your answers to a few questions?

When calling unannounced, especially on business executives, it is important to state a benefit before you begin to ask questions. Coming out of the blue from a stranger, a question is likely to be taken as meddlesome and be resisted with a natural reaction of, "It's none of your business." Even when that is not spoken it could be a reaction in thought.

A benefit gives people justification for sharing information in addition to sharing time of the day with you. Taking this approach also helps you avoid sounding impertinent by making wrong assumptions about their needs.

Your first objective with this type of opener is to determine whether or not you have a prospect. Your second objective is to assign a priority to your prospect. Here are four criteria that generally mark prospects:

1. They have a need for your product or service.
2. They can afford to pay for your product or service.
3. Potential volume justifies your time and effort.
4. They would be receptive to your presentation.

You need to prepare questions that will give you a picture of how they stack up with those four points. Chapters 8 and 9 cover probing techniques.

Close for an Appointment

After you give the benefit statement, the next part of your opener is to request an interview and a presentation. This could be scheduled immediately following the opener if the prospect's time allows and if other considerations suggest it's the right basis. Or you could set an appointment for another time. It's a good idea to let the prospect know approximately how long the appointment will take.

Putting It All Together

A complete opener with all three parts together would be:

Mr. Washington, my name is Pat Murphy with Acme Corporation. Mr. Washington, my special reason for calling on you today is to show you an idea that our customers tell us reduces hours of labor at least 20 percent on the assembly of gear boxes similar to the one on your model 102. You could evaluate this in about twenty minutes. Do you have the time now or would one o'clock this afternoon be better? *Do have to meet over coffe*

When closing for an appointment always be ready to take the initiative in suggesting a time and date. In the preceding example, instead of suggesting the specific time, supposing you had asked, "When would it be convenient for you to take a look at this idea, Mr. Washington?" It's a good bet you would get a reply something like, "Give me a call in a couple of months." At that time, your visit would be forgotten and you'd have to start from scratch.

Notice, too, in the last example, alternative choices of time were suggested. Alternate choices are one of those old sales techniques that have been around since day one of sales training. Some salespeople don't feel comfortable using them. If you don't, don't use them.

But, before you summarily reject alternate choices, stop to think about why they have been around so long and why they can still be effective when used properly. It is easier for someone to decide between two positives, rather than a positive and a negative. It is easier for prospects to decide *when* they will grant you an appointment, rather than *whether* they will grant you an appointment. Alternate choices are assumptive. You assume in your mind the prospect will grant you an interview. It's just a question of when. Your manner and the sound of your voice will have a more positive ring to them. You won't sound wishy-washy.

The main objection to using alternate choices is that when not properly spoken they tend to sound "canned." It sounds as if the salesperson memorized a technique. When using alternate choices, it's essential to make them sound naturally conversational with a spontaneous tone. We will get into the important nonverbal aspect of stating openers in Chapter 13.

If one of your alternatives is now, pause after you say, "now." Because if the prospect continues the dialog and carries the call into the interview or presentation stage at that time, you don't need an alternative time.

There was a time when sales reps were taught to schedule appointments at odd times such as 9:02 or 10:26. Stay away from such cutesy tricks. Reasonable, experienced buyers know you are doing it for effect. They don't like anything done to them for effect. Give them credit for knowing it's unlikely, when scheduling appointments, that nine o'clock or ten-thirty would make any difference.

When Prospects Want More Information

Prospects often will respond to your opener by asking questions such as, "What is this all about?" or "Could you tell me more about what this is?" They haven't yet agreed to set an appointment. Nor do they give any indication the dialog will be allowed to continue for any length. In fact, they seem to expect a one-liner for your answer so they can quickly decide whether or not to hear more.

Be prepared for this. So far you are still in the opener phase. Avoid saying anything that may cause unfavorable prejudgment. Don't begin a full presentation with anything less than what you know is the right basis. It helps when your presentation includes a demonstration or visual material. Then you can say:

Mr. Lincoln, I wish I could tell you all about it in just a word or two. But you will be able to evaluate it a lot faster by seeing it. It would take just twenty minutes for you to determine whether or not this would be profitable for your firm. Shall we do that now or would one o'clock this afternoon be better?

They may press you further, insisting on more detail. Try to phrase your answers by placing emphasis on what your product or service will do for them, rather than a description, even though they seem to press for the answer to "what is it?" You know in your heart that they are really not interested in that. They are interested only in the benefits it will provide.

Imagine an insurance agent selling a pension and profit-sharing plan. The prospect asks, "But what is it?" If the answer were simply, "life insurance," the door is likely to be closed very quickly with, "Not interested." At any given moment, most people are not interested in buying life insurance. But they would be interested in saving tax dollars. If it happens that life insurance is used to fund a tax-deductible retirement plan, that's fine. However, it is accepted as fine only after the tax-deductible benefits are understood. The agent is not doing the prospect a favor by answering the "what is it" question directly. That person may go through life never realizing how many needless tax dollars were being spent.

How to Use Referrals

Another good opener is a referral. Be sure you have permission to use the referrer's name and check to make sure the prospect will recognize it. On a business or professional call, it is best that your prospect can identify with the referrer in a similar business or professional situation and that the referrer is equal or higher in status. It wouldn't be a good idea to use the name of a low-ranked manager from a small company with a prospect who is a top-level executive of a large corporation. A referral would go something like this:

Mr. Jefferson, my special reason for calling on your this morning is at the suggestion of John Adams of the Adams Company. He's been a customer of ours for several years and is pleased with ideas we created especially for him that he said

helped develop some profitable new business. He felt sure you
would be interested in considering what we have to offer. . . .

One note of caution regarding referrals. Unless you have an
unlimited supply of them, don't get hooked on referrals. I've
known salespeople who are reluctant to make a new contact
without one. They also let a lot of good selling time slip by
while they are setting up referrals. Of course a referral is a
good way to introduce yourself to a stranger, but not the only
good way. You will be wise to use referrals as only one of
several approaches in your opening repertoire.

With or without a referral, know that most people you will
call on are basically courteous. They will be willing to devote
a few minutes of their time to a courteous and sincere stranger
who appears to offer at least an idea that could have merit.

Chapter 7

THE MAGIC DOOR OPENER

In this chapter we consider a variation to our opener that is especially effective with prospects who are complacent, who are satisfied, or who don't want to change.

AIDA Revisited

Some years ago, before many of the active salespeople of today were even born, a simple sales technique was taught throughout the land known as the AIDA formula. AIDA is an acronym that identified four steps, in their proper sequence, necessary to make a sale. Using this formula, you first need to gain the *attention* of the prospect to listen to you. The next step is to create *interest* in what you have to say. Then you build a *desire* for what you have to sell, and finally you call for *action* that closes the sale.

The only problem with the AIDA formula, if there was one, was overexposure. After years of expounding it in books and training sessions, it ultimately became old hat. It is interesting to note that the reasons, rooted in human nature, which made the AIDA formula effective never changed, because human nature hasn't changed. The only thing that changed was the attitudes of trainers, writers, and the salespeople being trained. Another side of human nature seems to propel us to abandon the wisdom of the ages and cause us to seek new, sophisticated, less commonplace wisdoms. The recent history of the organizational training movement is replete with fads that come and go. Actually, many of the newer fads are nothing but old hats with new ribbons.

Getting back to the AIDA formula, the reality is that you're just not likely to close a sale unless you build desire on the part of prospects. Likewise you can't build desire until you gain interest, and that doesn't happen without getting their attention.

The closed sale we are primarily concerned with in this book is sometimes referred to as the sale before the sale, that is, the time spent building sufficient desire on the part of a prospect to agree to listen to your sales presentation. All four steps of the AIDA process in opening situations are compressed into a matter of just a few minutes, sometimes even less than a minute. Therefore, you must come forth with the strongest attention and interest getter you can conceive in order to do the job quickly, not to overpower your prospects, but rather to appeal to their self-interest.

The Human Spark Plug That Ignites People to Action

To find a strong appeal, let's go back to the behavioral scientists who gave us the important insight in Chapter 5 that *all human behavior can be traced to a person's desire for a feeling of well-being*. Please take special notice of the word *feeling*. Human behavior is determined by emotion much more than by logic.

Now consider what happens when someone does not have a feeling of well-being. Recall the times when you were deprived of good feelings. Think of being too cold or too hot, hungry, thirsty, tired, bored, or otherwise uncomfortable. The more discomfort you felt in any of these situations, the stronger your urge to do something to relieve the feeling of discomfort and return to your feeling of well-being. In other words, the discomfort felt when a person is deprived of well-being or envisions possible loss of well-being is a powerful force that will propel that person to take action. This is important to consider when you want to gain the attention of someone who appears disinterested. The degree of interest will depend on the degree of relative dissatisfaction a person feels. Someone who feels satisfied will see no reason to change the present situation, and is therefore not interested in considering any action to cause it to change.

Let's go back to the buying motives matrix:

Gain	*Avoid*
Pride	Criticism or ridicule
Pleasure	Pain
Profit	Loss
Security	Fear or anxiety

Accentuate the Negative?

Motivating factors in the right-hand column are stronger than the ones on the left. Behavior aimed at avoiding the feelings on the right is more strongly motivated than behavior aimed at gaining or increasing the feelings on the left.

Let's compare the urge to avoid the emotional effects of criticism, ridicule, shame, or embarrassment with the desire to gain feelings of pride.

According to *The Book of Lists,* the number one fear of Americans is speaking to groups. Death is number six on the list. Isn't that amazing? People would rather die than speak in public! Why is it such a distressing fear? It's fear of criticism, ridicule, shame, and embarrassment. Once you get over that fear, it's easy. In fact, it's fun. I do it 150 days a year with relish despite the fact that at one time in my adult life, I couldn't lead a group in silent prayer.

Now take avoiding pain versus gaining pleasure. Ask a few people who smoke whether they would like to quit. When you hear yes, ask, "Why don't you?" Chances are you will hear, "I enjoy smoking."

But this usually is not true. With smokers who would like to quit but don't, the reason they don't is they can't stand the pain of withdrawal. For most smokers, what they think is pleasure is really avoidance behavior. The truth is, they continue smoking to avoid the withdrawal pain even though they want to quit. Therefore, avoiding pain or the discomfort they feel when they are deprived of smoking is a more powerful motivating force.

Let's try avoiding loss versus gaining a profit.

Suppose your phone rang at three o'clock on a cold rainy morning and a voice said, "Hey, there's someone in your front yard with a brand-new radial tire for your car. All you have to do is go out there and he will give it to you." You would probably slam the telephone back down and crawl back into bed mumbling about some kind of a nut out there.

But suppose your phone rang at three o'clock on a cold rainy morning and a voice said, "Hey, there's someone out on your driveway trying to rip off one of those brand-new radial tires you just had put on your car." Chances are you would want to throw on a pair of jeans and a raincoat and go out to stop him, wouldn't you? And that is true of most people. They are more strongly motivated to avoid losing what they already have than to gain a profit.

Anxiety is one of the most uncomfortable feelings we humans ever experience. A classic situation is found in parent and child relationships. A child misbehaves. The parent has a gnawing feeling in the pit of the stomach, thinking, "What am I going to do with this kid? How can I handle this kid?" The anxiety grows so strong that the parent becomes angry and yells at the child or strikes the child because anger is easier to bear than anxiety. We will do anything to get rid of it. Anger happens to be one of the most convenient ways to get rid of the feeling of anxiety. Often when you see someone who is angry, that someone is hurting. We use anger to drown out the hurt.

So when you have prospects who are complacent, satisfied, or reluctant to change, you must get them dissatisfied with their present situation. Whenever you call on strangers, it's a fact they have been getting along just fine without you. Had you never crossed their path, never in their lifetime would they ever have missed you! Ordinarily, they are not aware of any dissatisfaction at the moment you call.

Suppose you feel fine, everything is going great. A friend says, "I have this new headache remedy that just beats anything I've ever used." Your reaction is probably something like, "That's nice." It's just small talk. You would just as soon talk about something of livelier interest.

On the other hand, suppose you have a splitting headache. You would give almost anything to go home and go to bed but you have an appointment with your biggest customer, who is about to renew a contract. Tomorrow the customer leaves on a Caribbean cruise and you know that one of your competitors will be on that same ship. A friend says, "I have this new headache remedy that just beats anything I've ever used." You bet you're going to be interested!

Consider a third situation. You are feeling fine. Everything is going great. A friend says, "Suppose you have a splitting headache. You would give almost anything to go home and go to bed but you have an appointment with your biggest customer, who is about to renew a contract. Tomorrow the customer leaves on a Caribbean cruise and you know that one of your competitors will be on that same ship. Well now, I've discovered a new headache remedy that just beats anything I've ever used. And if you ever had a headache in a situation in which you just had to keep going, it would really save the day for you."

Your interest in the third situation may not be quite as high as it was in the second situation but it will certainly be a lot higher than it was in the first one.

Feelings are only temporary. They can be changed. Success in gaining the attention of a prospect often hinges on your ability to bring about an awareness of a dissatisfaction. Just as benefits do not exist unless they are in the mind of the prospect, feelings connected with the loss of well-being do not exist unless that person is actually experiencing or envisions such loss.

Remember Professor Harold Hill in the Broadway hit musical *The Music Man?*[8] Professor Hill toured the country selling band instruments and band uniforms. He had a good grasp of the principle of making people aware of problems they didn't know they had. The day he arrived in River City he saw a pool table being moved into a building owned by the local mayor. That evening when the citizens of River City were milling around the town square, Professor Hill went into a song and dance called "Ya Got Trouble." Using many vivid images, he convinced the people that the moral character of their whole town—and especially of their children—would be seriously threatened by the new pool hall.

In a four-minute song, he used the word *trouble* fifteen times. In chorus the townsfolk chanted the word *trouble* in the background over eighty times. How is that for getting attention? How is that for getting feedback from the prospects confirming their awareness of the problem?

Now everyone was keenly interested in hearing about a solution. And, of course, his solution was to have a boys' band. Their sons would be practicing every day after school instead of hanging around the pool hall. And wouldn't every mom be proud to see her son marching in a parade down Main Street in a fancy uniform and playing "Seventy-Six Trombones?"

Professor Harold Hill had a good grasp of the need to get people to envision the loss of feelings of well-being as an attention getter. He knew he didn't stand a chance of getting the folks interested in his merchandise until they first saw it as the remedy to big trouble.

Of course, Professor Hill was guilty of some exaggeration in dramatizing the trouble in River City. Perhaps it was done for the sake of adding an important piece of showmanship to a musical comedy. The example from *The Music Man* isn't used here to advocate dishonesty. Unfortunately, there are unscrupulous people who apply this principle to swindle others.

For instance, a local television news team runs an exposé of a basement waterproofing company that advertises for a free inspection of potentially leaking basements. Their "inspectors" are trained to tell all the prospects who respond to the ad that their basement walls are in danger of collapsing unless they are willing to spend several thousand dollars for a waterproofing job. You will find "furnace inspectors" who warn of defectless furnaces about to blow up and auto mechanics who sell unneeded repairs. I even remember a doctor who once pointed a warning finger at me as he said, "Get those tonsils before they get you!" Well, those tonsils are still in my throat many years later, thanks to another doctor who asserted that there clearly was no reason for them to be removed.

Yes, there are those who will tell lies to achieve selfish ends. Their shabby conduct need not restrain you from using truthfulness to help people become aware of real problems that stand in the way of a better life for them. The world is full of people with legitimate problems, people who need only honest and objective guidance to show them a better way.

The core insight in the River City example is the importance of bringing a clear mental picture of a problem to the center of your prospects' attention, getting them to agree that it is a problem, and getting them to realize that they are dissatisfied enough about it so that they want to consider how to resolve the problem.

Therein lies the magic door opener!

I like to use the phrase "trouble in River City" as a mnemonic device to remind me of what I need to do to get people's attention and spark their interest. I need to find their "trouble in River City" and talk about that first. I must be genuinely interested in their problem. At the attention-getting stage, what I have to sell is not even mentioned. It has no place in the conversation until their problem, their dissatisfaction is clearly in focus.

For example, follow me on a call on an executive of a company to sell a new sales training program. As often happens, I will spend some time in the reception lobby waiting until my prospect is ready to see me. Reception lobbies usually have magazine lying around and they present an opportunity to catch up on reading. I reach for one with a provocative headline on the front cover. But wait! My mnemonic device shifts into action. I remember that the important issue at hand is "trouble in River City." This company must have some problems. Its salespeople are probably missing some business in situations where they could be making sales. What are those situations? I look for company literature, brochures, catalogs. I ask the receptionist some questions about the products they sell. I try to relate all this new information with experiences I've had consulting with other companies in similar situations. When I finally get face to face with my prospect, my consciousness is totally involved with trying to find the "trouble in River City." It's the ideal mental state to slide right into my opening remark and then probe for the specific problem my prospect has.

Earlier I gave an example of a benefit statement I have often used when selling training programs. Let me now add a "trouble in River City" line to it: ". . . an idea that my clients tell me helps their salespeople to generate more new business—that helps them to get business in situations where they may have been missing it." I know that at least 95 percent of the sales executives feel that their salespeople aren't getting all the business they ought to be getting.

My prospects usually are not thinking of a problem at the moment I approach. I have to put a problem into the forefront of their mind before they will want to take the time to hear about a solution.

"Trouble in River City" is always the absence or opposite of your benefit. Here are a few examples:

Benefit	*"Trouble in River City"*
Make a profit	Miss out on profits
Cut costs	Waste money
Save time	Waste time and payroll dollars
Easier to do	Work harder than necessary
Save taxes	Overly generous to the government
Improve health	Risk poor health
Peace of mind	Worry, fear
Improve employee morale	Excessive employee turnover
Improve image	Avoid looking bad
Improve customer satisfaction	Avoid customer complaints

The list is endless, especially when you can relate "trouble in River City" to something specific that is going on in the prospect's world.

Write out a list of dissatisfactions your prospects and customers have for which you have solutions. Be as specific as you can to the problem situations you typically observe. Brainstorm with other salespeople. This makes good subject matter for sales meetings. If you sell to certain niche industries, read their trade magazines. The trade press is full of articles about common problems in each field. Attend their association meetings; common problems are often on the agenda. Compose openers with emphasis on "trouble in River City" in order to find your magic door opener.

Be careful not to overtly accuse a prospect of having a problem. That is another reason why the words ". . . our clients tell us . . ." can be advantageous. You are not making the accusation. Your prospect identifies with someone else who has a similar situation. More on how to stay out of trouble with "trouble in River City" is the subject of the next chapter.

To determine need for some products or services, it is helpful or even necessary to conduct an inspection of the prospect's operation or physical plant, to interview employees, or something of that nature. Bear in mind that many organizations spend big bucks for consultants to do what you are offering to do free of charge. This is a good spot for a "trouble in River City" opener. It would go something like this following the introduction part:

> Ms. Lincoln, we are working with many companies similar to yours that were amazed to discover the amount of money they were losing each day because of needless or improper maintenance. My special reason for calling on you today is to get permission to survey your operation to see if we can suggest some ideas that will reduce your maintenance cost.

Ways to Avoid Prejudgment

When prospects press you for further detail about the "idea" in your opener, tell them a story about one of your customers who struggled with a problem—how miserable he felt, how much money he was losing, how much "trouble in River City" there was. Then you came along. The sky cleared. The sun came out, and they lived happily ever after.

OK, you may think, that's a bit much. And for some situations, you may be right. But the classic storytelling formula is:

1. Here they were. (conflict, struggle, pain, problem)
2. Here is what they did. (solution)
3. Here they are now. (problem solved)

Billions of dollars are spent every year on advertising using that formula. You've seen the scenario hundreds of times. It goes something like this:

"What's the matter, Ed? You look down in the dumps."

"Well, you know, Charlie—pain, itch, swelling."

"Have you tried Formula X?"

"Does it really work?"

"It sure does. Doctors recommend it."

Next scene, another day:

"Gee, Charlie, you were right! The pain, itch, and swelling are gone. I feel like a new person thanks to you and to Formula X."

Take a tip from your advertising brethren. Go ye therefore and do likewise.

Please don't interpret up-front questions by prospects as being objections. Questions are a positive sign. It means you've struck interest. That's good. Curiosity is a powerful stimulant to interest. Curiosity may have killed many cats, but lack of it has killed many sales. Curiosity is a main reason prospects will listen to you at all. Do whatever you can to encourage it!

A Positive Approach

Some salespeople question the concept of "trouble in River City." They wonder if putting all that emphasis on someone else's problem might be considered a negative approach. The fact remains that when their mental awareness is attuned to avoiding criticism, ridicule, disapproval, pain, financial loss, and fear, most people are more strongly motivated to take action than when it is attuned to gaining pride, pleasure, profit, or feelings of security. Sure, it sounds nicer the other way around. And I'm certainly not a cynic. It is true that some are motivated for loftier reasons, and to think that everybody is at all times would be a nobler, however unrealistic, thought. But call after call, week in and week out, when it comes to human motivation, the odds are always in favor of avoidance behavior.

The end result of our effort is a solution to the problem. What could be negative about that? If you agree that people do things for their reasons, putting their problems in clear perspective gets them to realize that you are genuinely concerned about their reasons.

If you begin by talking about all the wonderfully positive things about your product, you will sound like so many other salespeople who have dollar signs in their eyes. Your prospects won't be interested in solving that problem! It's human nature that in order to get anyone interested enough to consider a solution, the problem must be clearly in focus first. No realization of a problem, no need to think about a solution.

Talk about aspirin would not be of much interest to people who feel good. But talk about aspirin when they have a headache, or envision the possibility of having one, brings about an entirely different level of interest. Recall the aspirin commercials on TV. They first show a person in pain, before aspirin comes into the picture.

I don't believe dissatisfaction is negative. I believe it is one of the most powerfully positive, creative forces in existence. If our ancestors had not been dissatisfied we would still be living in caves, wondering where our next meal was coming from. Dissatisfaction has released us from the drudgery of all kinds of back-breaking toil. Its creative force has given us all of the marvelous labor-saving conveniences that allow us to use our energies for even more creative pursuits. Dissatisfaction has eradicated the fear and heartbreak caused by diseases such as polio, tuberculosis, smallpox, and diphtheria. It is going to find a cure for cancer, find a substitute for oil as an energy source, and even figure out a way for nations to live at peace with one another.

Dissatisfaction negative? Not at all. We need more of it! And we need salespeople who are sowers of dissatisfaction. For if we have the highest standard of living in all human history, with an incredible volume and variety of comforts, luxury, convenience, and security, it is because in countless separate instances somebody sold somebody something.

Helping Prospects to Greater Satisfaction

Satisfaction and dissatisfaction are only states of mind. People often just think they are satisfied when in fact they are merely content to maintain the status quo. Remember the portion of Newton's First Law of Motion that states "any body in a state of rest will remain in a state of rest unless it is acted upon by some outside force." That's what selling is all about. It is the outside force that brings to light dissatisfaction with the status quo and moves people to enjoy greater satisfaction.

Think of the times you have approached prospects whose initial, knee-jerk reaction was "not interested," yet later at some point they bought from you. The need was present at the first contact but they simply were not aware of the need.

Most people are not completely satisfied at any given time. They don't have so much esteem, pleasure, profit, or security that they would not trade it for more esteem, more pleasure, more profit, or more security. To show the possibility of more satisfaction usually makes them dissatisfied with their present situation.

Turn a prospect's satisfaction into dissatisfaction by offering greater satisfaction.

Chapter 8

PROBING FOR NEEDS

Prince Dacun, the king's favorite son, lies dead on the battlefield. The young warrior Pion is given the swiftest horse to bring the message of the prince's death back to the king. All night Pion rides through hostile territory in a driving rainstorm, until the horse falls beneath him from exhaustion. At dawn he is captured by enemy soldiers and severely beaten. Since he is young and strong the soldiers decide to let him live and sell him as a slave. One night the soldiers drink too much wine and Pion escapes. On foot, traveling mostly at night in order to avoid capture, trudging over mountains, swimming through icy streams, fighting off wild animals, battered and exhausted, Pion finally makes it back to the palace to give the king the bad news. His reward? The king orders him beheaded!

This is an often-used theme dating back to Greek mythology. It reveals something about human response to bad news. Surely an exaggerated response by present-day standards of civilization, but it suggests a note of caution when confronting people with their problems.

If you are the bearer of bad news, especially if the news implies criticism of your prospect's efforts, chances are you will find, not your head, but the relationship cut off. In other words, you would be the one in "trouble in River City." Does this sound like a catch-22? On the one hand, we need to make people aware of their dissatisfactions, of their problems, of their needs. On the other hand, if we bring up these matters we put the relationship in jeopardy. But bring up these matters we must. Only we must do it tactfully.

How to Use Tact

The finest expression of tact in revealing your prospects' needs is to allow them to state their needs in their own words. The word *allow* is used here to make it clear that you subdue the temptation to directly state the problem yourself in a way that sounds accusatory even though the problem is obvious to you. People respond to their own words and ideas with far greater conviction than anyone else's. If they sense your words are based on your self-interest the response is sure to be negative. The best way to help people state their needs in their own words is through the skillful use of questions.

The counselor style of selling in vogue today places emphasis on probing for needs. Then a presentation is customized to fit the needs that are confirmed, rather than using a generic presentation that assumes every prospect has the same needs. But you can get into the counselor mode only when you establish credibility with a prospect. Answers to your questions may be confidential and not freely given to anybody who asks. And of course a prospect must spend some time with you to give you those answers. You must establish credibility verbally and nonverbally with an effective opener in order to qualify for the time and the information.

Preparing Questions for a Call

When I work with salespeople in the field, rarely do they prepare questions in advance of a call. Even when they understand that people do things for their own reasons, and understand the difference between features and benefits and the importance of emphasizing benefits, they still often make the mistake of immediately launching into a sales presentation based on what they think should be of interest to the prospect, instead of finding out. They plan the presentation in terms of what they are going to tell a prospect but rarely plan the questions they will ask.

Remember the TV comic playing the part of an oriental seer who can give answers before he knows the questions? If you try that routine on a call, your prospects may not think it's very funny—or relevant. The questions you ask can be more important than anything you say. Prospects may not believe the statements you make but they will certainly believe their own answers to the questions being considered. Unless you possess the capability of being adept at thinking on your feet, you will ask much more purposeful questions when you take the time to plan them carefully in advance.

And I do mean prepare them carefully. Often when the suggestion is made to salespeople that they prepare questions in advance, I observe this reaction, "Oh yes, let me see, I was supposed to think up some questions." Then there will be a hodgepodge of random questions for the sake of having some questions rather than questions designed to achieve a specific objective. This is another reason why call objectives are so important. If you know what you want to accomplish on a call, it is easier to design a game plan to accomplish your objective. Relevant questions are part of the game plan. Otherwise, you get the hodgepodge that leads only to frustration.

Questions Offer Many Benefits

Often when prospects say they're not interested, it doesn't necessarily mean that they're never going to be interested. It just means that at that time their minds are occupied with something else. But most people are conditioned to respond to questions and will when asked. Questions are an excellent way to break through this preoccupation barrier.

Skillful use of questions is the primary method of qualifying prospects—of determining if a suspect is a prospect. Answers to your questions and, sometimes more important, the manner in which they are answered give you clues to the priority each will be assigned and to the strategy you will use to convert these prospects into customers.

Asking questions affords an opportunity to get in tune with your prospects, to ascertain where they are emotionally and intellectually. You learn their language—words and phrases that are meaningful to them. Conversely, you will know what expressions may be unfamiliar to them and so avoid misunderstanding and the risk of being turned off.

Questions give prospects a greater sense of participation in an interview. People crave recognition. When used with skill, questions are an excellent form of giving recognition. With questions, you can make people feel important and let them know that you respect their opinions.

Turning Statements Into Questions

Some statements can be turned into questions by tagging them with, "Isn't it?" or "Do you agree?" or "What has been your experience with that?" For example:

"This is a new marketing opportunity for you, isn't it?"
"Many of our customers see an increasing demand for the bigger models. What has been your experience?"

In your own experience, who do you find to be the most interesting persons to talk with? Is it those who can captivate you with all the great things going on in their lives? Those who can dazzle you with all the wisdom they have on a variety of different subjects? Do you just sit and listen in amazement, utterly speechless? Or are you bored and somewhat peeved because you can't get a word in? Consider the nerd who went on and on about himself for a full hour. Finally he said to his companion, "Gee, I've been doing all the talking. How about you? What do you think of me?"

On the other hand, how do you feel about a person who asks questions about you, questions that take a benevolent tone of genuine interest in you and in what you feel free to reveal about yourself? Don't you find that kind of person a much more interesting partner in conversation?

Setting the Right Tone

The matter of tone is important, because questions asked for self-serving purposes can sound unfriendly, even threatening. Let's face it. There is a self-serving element in the salesperson's role. We set goals. We have call objectives that include making sales. Our livelihood, our jobs depend on that. We are held accountable if we don't. If we are not careful our self-interest will show through.

Questions can often raise doubts, make challenges, or imply disagreement with someone's point of view. Then too, remember the kind of questions parents and schoolteachers used to ask when your behavior and/or performance fell short of their preference.

Where have you been?
How many times do I have to tell you . . .?
When are you going to shape up?
Why did you do such a thing?

Stored in the recesses of everyone's memory are the feelings of guilt, humiliation, and lack of acceptance caused by such questions. You certainly want to avoid dredging up those feelings.

What Is Meant by Control

It is often said that questions should be used to control a sales interview. I believe *control* is an unfortunate choice of words. It carries with it connotations such as dominate, subdue, having it all one's way. This is exactly the opposite of what you want people to feel you are doing to them.

The other side of the control coin is a common notion on the part of salespeople that they "should be in control" of the sales interview, and that whenever they are not in control, they are demonstrating lack of competence.

This is an erroneous notion. If you ever have it, get rid of it. To believe you should be in control when you are not is going to trigger a downward emotional spiral. You will feel a twinge of anxiety in the pit of your stomach. This causes further loss of confidence. Then you lose some poise and, in fact, are not performing at your best. So now you've gone from a mental perception of lack of competence to the real thing. And it's needlessly self-imposed.

To me, this fallacy about a salesperson's compulsion to control a sales interview is a curious one. How absurd to think that you should be able to control a situation where the host is used to being in full control, and where you have a few minutes to start making sense before interest wanes and the host begins to look for ways to terminate the conversation. Who is going to be in control?

Initiative, I believe, is a better word than control. Asking questions is taking the initiative to establish the subject under discussion. Skillful use of questions keeps the discussion on track and provides the initiative to bring it back on track if it wanders in a different direction. Sometimes despite your best efforts it's going to wander beyond your ability to bring it back. If you've heard of legendary super salespeople who are able to control anybody every time, don't you believe it!

How to Eliminate the Prospect's Defensiveness

Selling has been characterized as an art in the sense that it is studied action and skilled execution in conducting a human activity. The essence of this skill is knowing and respecting the fine line between your goals and the prospect's goals. It is being effectively straightforward in asking purposeful questions that will allow you to apply your knowledge and experience in helping someone to identify a problem without putting that person on the defensive.

It will be helpful to get that fine line in focus if you examine your motives before planning questions to ask on a sales call. Are you trying to genuinely help someone find a better way? Or are you trying to be clever, to manipulate, to trick so you win, they lose? For if you do that, you are inviting defensiveness. You aren't going to help your own cause by putting prospects on the defensive.

The Kinds of Questions to Ask

You further lessen their defensiveness when you earn the right to ask questions. In the long term, you earn the right by becoming knowledgeable about your field. Remember the story of Fred Hawkins in Chapter 2. When Fred asks questions, his customers listen and are usually eager to answer because they recognize him as an expert who has valuable information to offer.

But on a more immediate basis, on a particular call, you earn the right to ask questions first by asking permission to ask some questions. Secondly, you reduce defensiveness by explaining why you are asking the questions. The reasons why, of course, are the prospect's reasons, not yours. For example:

Mr. Prospect, on the basis of our experience with other companies similar to yours, I believe we have some ideas that can lower your costs. But first I will need to know a few things about your operation so as not to make any wrong assumptions. Do you mind if I get your answers to a few questions?

In the interest of conserving time, so we can quickly determine if my ideas have an application here, could I get your answers to a few questions?

Closed-End and Open-End Questions

There are two types of questions you will want to consider using. Closed-end questions, sometimes called directive or fact-finding questions, are those that can be answered with a yes or no or simple statement of fact. Here are some examples of closed-end questions:

How many people do you employ?
Have you ever heard of our company?
What brand of product are you currently using?
When will you be receiving another shipment?
Who supervises this project?
Where is your head office located?
Does this sound reasonable to you?

It is a popular misconception that closed-end questions are only those that can be answered with a yes or no. Another part of the misconception is that all questions starting with "who," "what," "where," or "when" are open-end. Not so. Answer any of the preceding questions starting with those words. You will find the answer to each is a one- or two-word simple statement of fact. There is nothing more that needs to be said; therefore it is closed-end. The simple fact completely answers each question.

Open-end questions, sometimes called nondirective or feeling-finding questions, usually cannot be answered with a yes or no or a simple statement of fact. There is virtually no limit to the length of their answer, hence, open-end. Here are some examples:

How does this affect your business?
What is it you like about Brand X?
What is it you don't like about Brand X?
How do you feel about this?
Why is that important to you?
What directions will you be taking in this regard?

What kind of comments do you get from your customers regarding this product?

When to Use Closed-End Questions

▪ *To gather facts.* Are they interested in what you sell? Is there a budget for it? Who is the decision maker? Who else is involved in the decision? Are they currently buying your type of product or service from some other source? If so, who? The possibilities for fact-gathering questions are limitless.

▪ *To start a conversation.* Closed-end questions are easier to answer. The respondent is less guarded with them, therefore more comfortable and more willing to answer.

▪ *To gain attention.* As mentioned earlier in this chapter, most people are conditioned to answer questions and will when asked. Out of courtesy or habit, they will take their mind off their preoccupation at least momentarily to answer your question.

▪ *To draw out a silent person.* If you ever run into the quiet individual who is difficult to draw out, ask a closed-end question and then shut up. Even the sphinx-faced types can't stand silence for very long.

▪ *To change the direction of a conversation.* The opposite of the sphinx is a meandering, talkative gab. With this one you need to stop the rambling and get the conversation back to your agenda tactfully. You can usually interrupt someone if you ask a closed-end question about something he just said. As soon as it is answered with a yes or no or simple statement of fact, be prepared to jump right in and steer the conversation back on track.

▪ *To elicit preferred answers.* When your call objectives include getting specific information, planned closed-end questions can help you get that information quickly.

▪ *To clarify a point.* When someone says something and you're not sure what was meant, you can clarify the meaning by rephrasing the statement in your own words. Then ask if

that is what was meant. This is known as a paraphrase, which
will be covered in greater detail in Chapter 10.

- *To check interest.* Follow a statement you make by asking, "Would this be of further interest to you?"
- *To check understanding.* Follow a statement you make
by asking, "Does this make sense to you?"
- *To pinpoint a specific need.* This type of question is
sometimes called a nail-down question. It usually ends with a
contraction rather than the negative-sounding *not*. Use words
such as, "Wouldn't it?" "Shouldn't it?" "Isn't it?" "Doesn't
it?" For example, "A pre-planned program would save you a
lot of time, wouldn't it?"
- *To confirm an agreement.* This type of question is ended
with, "Is that agreeable with you?" or "OK?" sounding like
a question. Example, "I'll see you at 9:00 A.M. sharp, OK?"

When to Use Open-End Questions

- *To gather general information.* When you don't know
much about a prospect's situation and you are looking for a
specific area of need, or early in an interview, ask a question
something like this, "What has been your experience with
this type of product (or service) in the past?" You are more
likely to get in-depth information that helps you diagnose
needs—information you would not get from strictly closed-
end questions.
- *To uncover the emotional background.* Open-end questions are sometimes called feeling-finding questions. Inasmuch as people do things for emotional reasons, open-end
questions open the door for exploring this critical decision-
making emotional background. You gain not only factual
information, but also a view of the all-important opinions,
attitudes, and feelings which have so much bearing on their
actions. It is in these off-the-cuff verbalizations that your
prospects usually clarify their thinking, state their needs in
their own words, or give you a clue for paraphrasing their
statements, if necessary to further clarify an expression of
need.

Using the word *feel* in questions can be more effective than using the word *think*. For example, you could ask, "What do you think about that?" Better to ask, "How do you feel about that?" It is easier for people to talk about how they feel than about how they think.

- *To increase the prospect's participation.* Open-end questions are more conversational and involve more give and take. Prospects feel a greater sense of participation, less a sense of a salesperson giving them a "pitch."

- *To break up a series of closed-end questions.* When planning the questions you will ask on a particular call, be careful that you don't string too many closed-end questions in sequence. It can be a source of irritation for a person to answer a steady flow of closed-end questions. It can sound like some sort of unpleasant inquisition, such as a third-degree or witness-stand interrogation. How does this dialog between a hardware rep and a retail chain buyer sound?

Rep: Do your stores carry metal-cutting drills larger than ⅜ inch?

Buyer: Yes.

Rep: How large do they go?

Buyer: One inch.

Rep: Do you handle star drills?

Buyer: No.

Rep: How about taps in sets?

Buyer: Yes.

Rep: Individual taps?

Buyer: Yes.

Rep: Metric sizes?

Buyer: Yes.

Compare that commentary with this one:

Rep: Can you tell me something about the kind of drills, taps, and star drills you carry?

Buyer: Why, yes. Many of our stores are in smaller towns in rural areas. Farmers need heavy-duty, industrial-quality tools. So we stock larger sizes than stores in cities catering to primarily the do-it-yourself trade. Besides the farmer, we also serve local industries since they usually don't have convenient access to an industrial supply firm. Here again, we carry a good supply of large sizes, metric sizes, and individual pieces for replacement purchases in addition to sets. You mentioned star drills. Our stores carry them but purchase of all concrete tools is handled by the paint purchasing department.

The first example was six closed-end questions. The second example was one open-end question that elicited a lot more valuable information in a much more congenial atmosphere.

Sometimes you may have to ask several closed-end questions to draw out the specific information you need. In such cases, break the sequence with an occasional open-end question to loosen up the dialog.

The Importance of Balance

In my seminars, I often have salespeople write out a list of questions they ask on three different categories of calls: (1) new prospects, (2) prospects called on before who are giving all or most of their business to a competitor, and (3) current customers. For several years I kept track of the kind of questions listed. Ninety-four percent were closed-end questions.

Of course, closed-end questions are important. They provide much-needed factual information in addition to being useful for the other reasons stated earlier. But sales will be made easier and more often with judicious use of open-end questions.

Be especially mindful of using an indirect approach with your questions to encourage prospects to start talking about their needs. Bear in mind that it is not enough for you to find out prospects' needs. It is important that they discover what their needs are.

When They Are Buying From a Competitor

If you sell a product that gets repeat sales from buyers, you probably have prospects who are buying from competitors and are susceptible to change through a better idea. One thing you don't want to do is directly knock the competition. That implies that the buyer made a mistake and will tend to cause defensiveness.

An indirect approach allows prospects to arrive at a notion that it would be a good idea to evaluate their present source. And there you are ready to help them follow through on their own notion.

Begin your probing for needs with a closed-end question. Such questions are easier to answer and provide for a warm-up to the more thought-provoking, feeling-finding, open-end questions.

Suppose you were calling on a feed manufacturer to sell packaging. These would not be good questions with which to start the interview: "Do you need any bags today?" "Do you have need for lower packaging costs?" It would be better to go about it indirectly:

You: How many fifty-pound bags do you ship in a month?
Prospect: About 150,000.
You: How much are you paying per bag?
Prospect: Let's see, here's an invoice. Looks like seventeen cents per.
You: How do you feel about that price?
Prospect: Well, it's been going up like everything else. I guess it's getting to be more than I'd like to pay.

Now you have uncovered a need—dissatisfaction with the price being paid to a present supplier. The need was uncovered indirectly, in a way that made it easier for the prospect to reveal and less likely to deny later.

Of course, you would take this tack assuming you had some ideas about lower-cost packaging. Once a need is isolated in the interview, you know what direction your presentation must take to make a sale. You will build it around benefits that relate to the need.

Changing the Style of Questions

A closed-end question can be turned into an open-end question by the way it is phrased. Here are some examples:

Closed: Do you use word processing equipment?
Open: To what extent do you use word processing equipment?
Closed: Do you have any problems with that machine?
Open: What is your experience with that machine?
Closed: Do you like to travel?
Open: How do you feel about traveling?

Some closed-end questions can be tagged with an open-end question simply by following up with "Why?" or "Why is that?" or "Why is that important to you?"

How to Ask Why

Why is one of the most difficult questions for adults to ask. For the first few years after they learn to speak, little children don't seem to have any trouble with it. Later they learn that voices of authority, parents, teachers, and bosses often get impatient when responding to a why. At times the answer comes out, "Because I said so, that's why!" They learn that to avoid arousing a negative emotion, they shouldn't ask why.

Furthermore, we were taught not to be nosy, not to pry into other people's business. But in the business of selling, we need to do a certain amount of tactful, judicious prying.

Unless we know why people do what they do, or say what they say, we have no way of knowing how to proceed. We could waste valuable time going off in wrong directions, or we could miss opportunities that would benefit both the prospects and us because we didn't understand their hidden feelings.

When you ask why, it is important not to imply any judgment such as criticism or disapproval of the other person's position. Often this kind of judgment shows up in your tone of voice, a raised eyebrow, a squint, a hand gesture. If these come across in a way that suggests you disagree, you will be sure to trigger defensiveness on the part of your prospect. These nonverbal signals just happen unconsciously.

Keep in mind your motives for asking questions. If it is to manipulate, to attack, to trip up a prospect for your reasons, then you will tend to reveal that nonverbally. But if you are in full realization that the number one priority is to help someone find a better way, you won't need to be concerned about your body language. Instead, you can concentrate on the matter at hand.

Here are some alternative questions that have a softer sound:

- Obviously you have a good reason for saying that. Do you mind telling me what it is?
- What do you have in mind?
- How do you feel about this?
- How do you arrive at your decisions?
- What factors determine your decisions?
- If I knew what factors determine your decisions, I could be more specific. Could you tell me?
- Could you elaborate on that?
- Could you give me some examples?

Or simply ask for permission to ask why:

- Do you mind telling me why?

Consumer advertising campaign approaches are sometimes based on in-depth motivation research. An important technique researchers use is what is known as testing the extremes—that is, finding out what people like and what they don't like. You can borrow some of their methodology in conducting your own in-depth research.

For example, if a prospect is using a competitive product, you could ask: "What is it you like about that product?" Listen for the answer. Then ask, "What is it you don't like about it?" Again listen. Now you have some important information. Perhaps you can provide greater satisfactions in whatever it is he likes. Or you may be able to help him avoid something he doesn't like. Besides, you are not putting yourself in the position of knocking the competition. The prospect told you in what way the competitor is lacking.

Questions to Avoid

Whatever you do, please don't ask questions in an opener that have such blatantly obvious answers that they sound more like scolding and are sure to offend, such as:

- You do want to lower your costs, don't you?
- You do want to safeguard your family's health, don't you?

With questions like these two in an opener, you are likely to offend prospects. And their reasons will be emotional, having nothing to do with the logical merits of what you sell. You can't offend and persuade at the same time. Those questions may be all right in a summary statement when you are closing a sale, but please, not in an opener.

A Powerful Mind Opener—And Other Ways to Pinpoint Needs

There is an inoffensive way to phrase questions that will prompt people to admit they could be receiving an important

benefit or at least that you have something worth looking at.
It is an effective way of keeping a prospect's mind open when
it is heading toward a closed direction. It is known as the
contingency question, sometimes called the just-supposing
question. With this method you suggest a hypothetical situation and ask if a benefit would result from it or if it would be
worth considering. For example:

- Just supposing you had a machine that could perform this
  operation. Would it appreciably lower your costs?
- Just supposing there is an important new discovery that
  thousands have acclaimed to be an important safeguard
  to their family's health. Would you be willing to take
  fifteen minutes to learn about it?

Just supposing you took the time to list all the benefits your
customers enjoy as a result of buying from you. And just
supposing you did some creative brainstorming and composed
"just supposing" questions to go with each one. Wouldn't
that give you more opportunities to present your offering on
a more favorable basis?

In addition to asking questions, another indirect approach
to helping people discover their needs is to bring in a third
party. This could be a quote from a person likely to be
respected by your prospect or an article from a newspaper or
magazine. It could be a story about another person, perhaps
one of your customers who struggled with a problem until
you came along and solved it. Let your prospects identify
with the third party. Thus it is not you who suggest that they
have the same problem.

When newspapers and magazines want to draw attention to
a problem they wait until somebody does something about it,
then tell the story. Throughout history the most effective
communicators were storytellers. The Bible is full of stories
and parables that bring concepts to life. Most people would
rather hear stories about other people than about things or
abstract concepts.

When you finish your third party's story or statement, ask an open-end question such as:

- How do you feel about this?
- What has been your experience in this regard?

Quoting other people is an especially effective way of making what you say believable. It doesn't put you in a position of taking a stand that needs to be defended. Rather, you are in the position of a reporter relating what someone else said. Your prospects are less likely to disagree since you are attributing the remark to a neutral third party who is not there to sell something. However, if they happen to disagree, you can respond noncommittally with such remarks as, "Oh," or "Really," or "Hmm," and thus avoid getting into an argument. Instead, you can take another tack.

Keep your eyes and ears alert for quotes and stories. Read trade publications in your industry and your customer's industry with an eye for quotes and articles that are relevant. The more you do it, the more interested you become and your antennas become more finely tuned. Speaking of telling stories and asking questions, do you remember Anna Mae Randall, Harriet, Ed Posnan, Jim Tucker, Bob Komasinski, Hotshot Charlie, Fred Hawkins, Jerry Clement, Professor Harold Hill, and Pion the warrior? Did they help you get a better handle on some abstract concepts? How do you feel about that?

Remember to be tactful in helping others become aware of their needs. You use tact when you quote a third party, tell a story, or ask questions in such a way that prospects state their needs in their own words.

A Quick Qualifier

Here is an opener with an up-front qualifying question. It is especially adaptable to use on the telephone when you have an inkling of a possible need. At this point in my career, my best prospects are scattered all over the country. There are more of them than I could ever possibly reach. In order to make most effective use of my time, I need to qualify them quickly and allocate my time to situations that would be mutually most beneficial.

In this case I am selling a training program on Successful Cold Call Selling. After my introduction and benefit statement similar to the ones given in earlier chapters, I continue with something like this:

> Ms. Prospect, I'm not sure whether or not my ideas would apply to your business. But let me get your answer to a question. And if your answer is yes, it's not likely that it would apply. But if your answer is no, it would be beneficial for both of us to ask each other some questions to see if we should pursue it further. My question is this. Are you satisfied with the amount of new business your salespeople are presently generating?

If the answer is yes, it is immediately determined this is not a high-priority situation. But if the answer is no, the dialog usually continues with further qualification on both sides.

It's not to say that in your case a yes answer automatically disqualifies the prospect. Remember, for all practical purposes, I'm operating from an unlimited prospect base. At first blush some people, out of defensiveness, will throw you a smokescreen. And you may have a more limited base of high-quality prospects. Even so, with this opener you put the spotlight on a possible need very quickly. You have opened up the dialog. With a yes answer you may be able to continue with a further probe such as, "To what do you attribute your success?"

At this point prospects may not even know what you are selling. All they know is they have a pain and someone wants to listen—someone who may have had some experience and expertise in dealing with that kind of pain.

Let's apply this opener to your situation. Go back to the list of dissatisfactions you wrote out in the preceding chapter.

Insert your most commonly used ones into this question: "Are you satisfied with . . .?"

- What you are paying for . . .
- The time it takes you to . . .
- The time it takes your employees to . . .
- Amount of sales as a result of . . .
- Profits generated by . . .
- Return on investments from . . .
- Service . . .
- Delivery . . .
- Location . . .
- Employee turnover . . .
- Inventory turnover . . .
- Taxes you are paying . . .

Again the list is endless. Translate the general terms above into something as specific to the prospect's world as you possibly can. For example, if you sold or leased prestigious commercial property, and you knew your prospect was in a less desirable neighborhood, you could say, "Are you satisfied that your location is conducive to the image you want to portray in the community?"

When asking questions like this, make sure that your manner and the tone of your voice are not smug or accusatory. At this point you are not selling anything yet. You are not bragging about the fabulous property, or products, or services you have to sell. The prospect became aware of a pain, a dissatisfaction. You are an expert in dealing with that type of pain because of the experience you and your company have had with many other clients who have faced and struggled with similar types of pain. And you are willing to take time out of your busy day to listen to the prospect's pain.

There is an old cliché in selling that says, "Sell yourself first. Then sell your product or service." I say, "Find the pain first and become an expert on reducing pain." That is the best way to sell yourself!

Too often salespeople are quick to launch into a presentation that smacks of bragging about how great their product or service is. This is what prospects expect because it is what they see and hear all too often. Their conditioned response is to take it in with a grain of salt, which only reinforces their satisfaction with the status quo. The salesperson exits with a call made but little hope for a sale. Let your competition do that.

How to Perfect Your Skill

Asking questions requires skill. To be consistently successful in cold call selling, it is more important to be mentally alert for possible needs, and to be skilled in probing for needs, than it is to be a smooth-talking presenter. Like any other skill it will improve with practice. But don't confine your practice only to selling situations. Get in the habit of asking questions in all of your interpersonal contacts with friends, family, and fellow employees. Plan to spend some time with others, in a social evening or luncheon, when you make a special effort to avoid talking about yourself. Instead, ask questions that will communicate sincere interest in the people you are with. Keep in mind the suggestions in this chapter. Your companions will find you to be a much more interesting conversation partner. You will feel better about asking questions and about your improved communication skill.

Chapter 9

LISTENING— THE OTHER SIDE OF A QUESTION

In Chapter 8 the importance of asking questions was emphasized. Listening is the other side of questions. Unless the asker listens, the questions have no meaning.

A Lesson Learned Too Late

Glen Mobrey was in a state of utter shock. After twenty years of what he thought was a successful marriage, his wife asked him for a divorce.

"Well, we had the usual little disagreements," he related. "Doesn't everybody? But I hadn't the slightest inkling Dee was so unhappy that she wanted to call it quits. You know. I worked extra hard to earn the kind of money to give her everything I thought she ever wanted. But I didn't realize until it was too late that I didn't give her the one thing she really wanted above all the rest. I just didn't listen to her."

A Lesson Learned in Time

One of the greatest lessons I ever learned was taught to me by my daughter, Jill, when she was sixteen. I was known as a tough disciplinarian in those days. "Saturday night curfew is midnight," I would pronounce. "Not 12:15 or even 12:05, because if it were 12:05 I would have said 12:05 instead of midnight."

One warm summer evening it wasn't until a few minutes to 1:00 A.M. when a car finally pulled into the driveway. Her date must have seen me standing on the porch, under the light, with my arms sternly folded. He wasted no time shifting into reverse and screeching out of the driveway.

Jill gave me a cheery "Hi, Dad," as she lilted into the house. I was ready to go into the riot act routine but for some strange reason I kept my mouth shut. We sat down in the living room and she began to tell me all about her evening— what other kids did, what they said, how they felt, what was important to them. I hardly said a word except to respond to what was being said and ask some questions to clarify what I couldn't understand. It was a most absorbing conversational experience for me.

"Holy cow!" I finally said, "it's after three, and we've got to get up for church tomorrow. By the way, you know you were late."

"Yes, I guess so."

"What do you suppose we should do about that?"

"I suppose I should get grounded for a while."

Well, I don't think she ever was grounded as a result of that night. But the next morning she said to her mother, "Gee, Dad and I really had an interesting talk last night."

Interesting for me? Oh, yes! I got to know my daughter and to understand her generation in new and important ways. But over and above that, I learned how vital it is to a relationship to take the time to shut up and listen.

An Important Aspect of Communication

Have you ever had people ask you questions and it became obvious to you they were not listening to the answer? To make matters worse their eyes were flitting around to other sights and sounds they didn't want to miss. How did you feel about that?

Sorry I can't be there to listen to your answer to my question, but it's fairly safe to assume you don't feel very good about people who treat you that way. It is also safe to assume that your prospects are not going to feel very good about salespeople who don't actively and diligently demonstrate their willingness to listen.

In the Bible there's a story about Samson killing 10,000 Philistines with the jawbone of an ass. Every day thousands of sales are killed with the same weapon—by salespeople who won't shut up and listen.

Whenever I deal with the subject of communication in my seminars, I ask my audience what they would like to learn from that session. These are typical answers:

- How to make a presentation
- How to write effective letters
- How to speak to a group
- How to use humor
- How to talk on the telephone
- How to convince people who disagree
- How to handle complaints
- How to reprimand unsatisfactory performance

Almost never does anyone expect to learn something about listening. Yet, that is the subject of a major portion of my seminar presentation. Communication is a two-way street. In oral communication, listening is 50 percent of the action.

Attitudes More Important Than Skills

There are skills that can be taught to help people listen more effectively. But before skills learning can take place, communication trainees must first become aware of the need to improve listening skills. Secondly, they must cultivate a sincere willingness to listen.

Several organizational training directors have told me about their experience conducting comprehensive listening skills training programs. They would spend days practicing the skills. It was drill, drill, listen, listen. By the time the course was finished they were up to their eyeballs in listening. The last thing they wanted was to do more listening. Yet without *wanting* to listen, these skills are practically useless.

Listening appears to be a passive process. After all, everybody has two ears. Just do what comes naturally. What's the big deal?

The deal is that we talk at a rate of approximately 150 words per minute, but we can think close to 600 words per minute. That means that when someone talks to you, if you do what comes naturally, you will be thinking more words than you hear. It is easy to become distracted. It is easy to pursue a line of thinking other than what your conversation partner is leading up to. To follow a natural inclination is to be thinking of what you are going to say next. If you are not careful you are apt to miss some of what is being said. In a sales situation, what you miss could be indispensable information. To make matters worse, the prospect is likely to sense that you're not really listening, because doing what comes naturally is to nonverbally reveal what is going on inside of you. If you are impatient, bored, eager to express disagreement, or allowing your mind to wander, your prospect will know it. Result—the relationship is in jeopardy.

How to Listen Actively

So to avoid missing relevant information, to avoid jeopardizing relationships, be an active listener. Go beyond "doing what comes naturally" and make a deliberate effort to listen. Honestly try to gain an understanding of what is being said and of the feelings behind it. Show by your gestures and facial expressions that you are genuinely interested. Look at the person talking to you. Resist any temptation to shift your gaze to anything else that may be going on nearby. Take advantage of the extra thinking time afforded by the 450-word difference between speaking and thinking and use this time to concentrate on what is being said. Use it to review and collect the bits and pieces together into a central idea. Use it to determine what is being omitted—to understand the feelings underlying what is being said.

If you do all of this, you certainly will avoid the fatal error of interrupting a person in the middle of a thought. The only people who don't mind being interrupted in the middle of a sentence are prisoners.

At this point you may be thinking, "Hey, Lee, I buy what you say about listening. It sounds good in theory, but what about prospects who ramble on with irrelevant detail or who switch from one point to another? It's hard to make any sense out of what they are saying. Then the time they are willing to spend with you runs out before you get an opportunity to state your case."

Yes, that does happen, perhaps more often than we would like. We can lessen our distress in these situations knowing that we have established rapport with a prospect by being a good listener and that we left the door open for a return visit.

This line of reasoning makes more sense with telephone contacts than it does with personal calls. Personal calls are expensive. If the call is away from the home base or off the beaten track, it could be a long time before that prospect is going to be available to see you on a return visit. Then there is a matter of timing. By the time you get back there the competition may have become entrenched, the prospect's needs may have changed, or any of a number of things could have happened to lessen your advantage.

Even though are you faced with a person who rambles on, be a good listener. Make a conscious effort to avoid showing impatience, boredom, or indifference. Wait for a completed thought or a break in the monolog. Then unobtrusively direct the conversation back in line with your objective. If you fail in the first attempt, listen intently for the next chance.

Another way to exercise initiative in setting the direction of a conversation is to ask a closed-end question pertaining to something the prospect said. Be ready to pick up the conversation as soon as the answer is given. Tie your remark to the answer. Then use it as a transition back to the point you want to discuss.

For example, let's suppose you are selling an advertising program that is built around a promotion to build store traffic for merchants in a shopping center. Halfway through your opening remarks to a prospect, let's call him Mr. DeBate, he interrupts you to go off on a tangent about the lack of business caused by "those stupid politicians running the government and their idiotic economic programs." While DeBate has the floor, your advertising program is out the window and politics is in.

Mr. DeBate ends a sentence with, "And I'll never vote for him again." Here's the cue for you to jump in quickly with your closed-end question.

"I take it you voted for him in the last election?"

"Yes, unfortunately."

"Well," you pick up, "I guess we're stuck with him till the next election but I don't think it's a good idea to let the things we can't do prevent us from doing the things we can do. Now, we can't get rid of this administration for a while, but we can do something constructive to stimulate business in our own backyard and that's the reason I'm here, Mr. DeBate. . . ." Then get back to the purpose of your call.

You gave Mr. DeBate a chance to release some pent-up feelings. You gave him the courtesy of listening to his point of view without letting it get too far out of hand. You discreetly changed to another subject that should be of interest to him. Now he is more likely to return the courtesy and hear you out.

Make the Most of Your Presence

Your biggest advantage when you're in the presence of a prospect is that you are already there. You have surmounted the tasks of getting through any screen of receptionists, secretaries, or assistants. The prospect is not out of town, in a meeting, or otherwise preoccupied. You don't have to arrange an appointment or work at getting attention. All of this is an accomplished fact. Do what you can to make the most of having completed all of those steps.

In other words, don't be too quick to settle for merely establishing rapport and leaving the door open for a return visit. This visit may be your best opportunity.

Good listening takes awareness. It takes skill, and as with any skill, it takes practice. At the end of the last chapter, it was suggested that you practice asking questions in social situations. Now include the ideas from this chapter in your social practice experiences. Especially notice how positively people will respond to your willingness to let them be heard. There are millions of people with a deep craving to have somebody share their thoughts and feelings, to be understood, to know that someone appreciates them enough to listen to them for a few minutes. Give them what they want. They will want to have you around. They will give you their friendship—and very often their business.

Chapter 10

PARAPHRASING

In this chapter you will learn *paraphrasing*, a technique that many salespeople tell me proved to be the most valuable addition to their sales skills repertory they ever learned—one that dramatically changed their status in the sales profession from just OK to top producers in an amazingly short time. The reason for their quantum leap to success came from a newly acquired ability to set up presentations under the best of circumstances with prospects who responded to an opener with indifference, yet had very important problems that needed to be solved.

The Technique of Paraphrasing

To paraphrase in selling is to rephrase a prospect's statement with words that will reveal unexpressed meanings and feelings lying hidden beneath the original statement. These unexpressed meanings and feelings often give clues to a need.

The paraphrase clarifies the language. It brings the need out into the open and gets the prospect to agree that it is a need.

You will find the technique is easy to learn if you have grasped the essence of Chapters 5 through 9. It has always been a source of wonder to me why I find so few salespeople who know about this powerful technique, let alone who use it to good effect. All too often high-priority prospects with real needs, wants, problems, and dissatisfactions are written off at their first expression of indifference. Yet these often turn out to be the best long-term customers. Competition for their time and attention is less because so few other salespeople get through to them. This technique can be used on the telephone as well as in person.

In Chapter 8 it was suggested that the finest expression of tact in revealing your prospects' needs is to allow them to state a need in their own words. Rarely will someone come right out and in explicit, concise words articulate a need that can be satisfied by what you sell. More often you get bits and pieces or vague generalities that merely hint at possible needs. Sometimes you even hear an attempt to cover up a real problem.

Those bits, pieces, generalities, and cover-ups are signals for you to go on the alert. Focus your concentration on applying all the Chapter 9 listening skills. In particular, listen to identify feelings that lie hidden beneath the words you hear. Try to fill in the blank spaces of what is being omitted. The generalities are also a cue for using the questioning skills from Chapter 8 to reduce vague statements to something specific.

On a first call, the prospect is often preoccupied with other matters and therefore indifferent to what a salesperson may want to discuss. The best way to change the attitude of indifference to one of interest is to ask questions until a need, a problem, or a dissatisfaction is uncovered.

Once a need is revealed, the next step is to suggest a benefit your product or service offers that will satisfy the need. Then if a complete presentation is necessary, suggest doing that on the spot or set an appointment for a future presentation date.

Change "Too Busy" Into "Better Find Time to Look"

One of my clients is a manufacturer of automated livestock feeding systems sold primarily to dairy farmers. These systems greatly reduce the labor a farmer must put forth to feed a herd. Tim Wall, a salesman for the company, recalled a dialog he had with a farmer on a new prospect call. Tim no sooner introduced himself and identified the company he represents than the farmer looked up from the machine he was repairing and declared, "Sorry, I'm not going to have time to talk to you. Just too much work to do around here."

"You've got a pretty big operation. Do you work it all by yourself?" Tim asked a closed-end question in order to learn an important fact.

"Yes."

"How do you manage to get all those chores done by yourself?" Tim probed further with an open-end question.

"I tell you, it's rough. My son went away to college this year so it's the first time I'm alone since we got so big. It's hard to find a dependable hired hand around here, so I guess I'll just do what I have to do."

"It seems to me you would like to figure out a way to cut down on some of these chores and still produce the same amount of milk. And that's what you really want, isn't it?" Tim paraphrased.

"Yes, I suppose so," the farmer agreed.

"That's great," Tim replied, "because my special reason for calling on you this morning is to meet you and arrange an appointment for a time, at your convenience, when you can take a look at an idea that many dairymen find cuts their feeding chores in half. Could we do that this evening, or would tomorrow be better?"

How Background Information Helps Chart the Course

Needs are fairly predictable in most selling situations. If you are selling a product like Tim's that offers the latest labor-saving technology and the prospect is using obsolete equipment, the need is probably obvious to you. If you are selling a financial service that offers tax breaks of which your prospect is not taking advantage, again, the need is obvious to you but perhaps not to the prospect.

It is helpful to get as much preliminary information about each prospect as possible. Tim Wall had the advantage of being on the scene of the problem. He could tell with his experienced eye that the ancient silo and obsolete equipment spelled "trouble in River City." When he found out that it was being worked by only one man, that meant even bigger trouble. Tim's objective, then, was to arrange a time when he could tell his whole labor-saving story under the most advantageous conditions.

Tim had heard that "I don't have time to talk to you" routine many times before. He knew that kind of statement is just an unthinking reaction, not a firm position. Furthermore, he realized the best way to meet his objective was to get the prospect to feel that it was his own idea to take the time to listen.

Paraphrasing allowed Tim to clarify the language and so put the need in recognizable, concrete terms. Even though the farmer didn't choose the very words Tim used in his paraphrase, for all practical purposes he felt they were his. He in fact agreed that what Tim said was what he meant. His agreement was a perfect entrée for Tim to offer to show him an idea that would be worth taking the time to think about as a solution to his problem.

The comments you hear in the early phases of a contact with a new prospect that reflect indifference usually sound something like this:

- "I'm not interested."
- "I'm too busy to see you."
- "I don't want to get into that now."
- "We are satisfied with our present source of supply."
- "Not going to spend any money now."
- "Call me in a couple of months."

All too often, salespeople take these comments at face value, terminate the contact, and go look for another prospect. In other words, they are just out cherry picking.

Paraphrasing Cushions the Bluntness

Even when they do hang in there, a common mistake salespeople often make is to come back with a blunt question that has a blatantly obvious answer, which was advised against in Chapter 8, such as: "You do want to make more profit, don't you?" "You do want to cut your costs, don't you?" "You do want to safeguard your family's health, don't you?"

Questions like this are sure invitations to rejection. They are accusatory. Prospects become defensive about them. You get drawn into an argument you may win in logic, but you will lose an opportunity to make a sale.

It is contrary to human nature for anyone to suddenly switch from "I'm not interested," or any other such objection to "Yes, I am interested and will listen to your presentation" on the basis of such blunt questions.

Paraphrasing allows the prospect a face-saving opportunity to make a more graceful change of mind. When Tim Wall used a paraphrase, it took more than a blunt question for the dairy farmer to switch from "Sorry, I'm not going to have time to talk to you" to agreeing it would be worth considering.

Besides being blunt, questions used in the examples four paragraphs ago are too abstract—too far removed from an immediate problem a prospect can "feel in the bones."

Get the Main Issue Up Front

In earlier chapters we considered feelings like empathy and how deep is the craving of people to be understood. The best kind of understanding takes place at levels of immediate, real-world experience—specific situations you can point to. It has often been said that people don't buy because they understand your product or service as much as they buy because they feel you understand them. When you paraphrase, you prove to the prospect that you listened, you understood, and you considered what was said important.

Paraphrasing gives you a vehicle to translate general statements into something specific that prospects can identify as being a problem of immediate concern. Thus, they are more likely to give it higher priority in addition to getting a stronger feeling that you understand them.

Realize, then, as Tim Wall did, that initial objections are not firm stands or even the main issue. The main issue is that you have something that will benefit your prospects—that will satisfy specific needs. To get this main issue to be the topic of conversation you must first isolate the need. Then you want your prospects to *agree* that they recognize it. Like the River City townfolk in *The Music Man,* they are singing along with you that there is "trouble in River City."

Now they are in the best frame of mind to consider your solution. At this point of agreement, tell of a benefit that relates to the need you've identified and ask for an opportunity to make a full presentation.

When the dairy farmer agreed that it sure would be worth thinking about a way to cut down on some of his chores, Tim came right back with the suggestion that he had something which was proven to do just that. Then he asked for an appointment.

It is usually difficult and unlikely for anyone to refuse to hear your full presentation when a strong need is hanging out there in bold relief and an opportunity to take a look at a solution is being offered.

Sometimes after a paraphrase, a realization begins to dawn that the need you exposed is greater than the prospect was at first willing to admit. It can take some time for the full realization to sink in. All the while he may be hesitating to agree to an appointment, but still he can't give you a straight-out no. This is when it pays for you to hang in there, especially in the case of a business need. For to ignore it is fraught with risk that could spell big trouble for a business prospect.

I hope we've laid to rest any reluctance to bring needs, problems, or dissatisfactions out into the open. The truth is, we do a great disservice to our clientele if we do not use our persuasive skills to help them find a better way.

Giving Prospects Valuable Perspective

Business people, especially, become so engrossed in the routine details of running their business that they often fail to see needs that are obvious to an outsider. There is an old saying, "Important things are put aside for the urgent until the important things become urgent and then sometimes it is too late." You can help people to put things in their proper perspective, and to take action on some important things before they become urgent.

Keep in mind that the purpose in paraphrasing is to bring out into the open unspoken needs, wants, problems, or dissatisfactions. If a problem is stated directly by a prospect, there is no reason to paraphrase. In such a case simply tell of a benefit that relates to the problem and close the sale. Or when a complete presentation is necessary, ask for an opportunity to do so.

How to Start a Callback

When you set an appointment to make the presentation at a future date, be sure to begin the callback with a restatement of the need and again get an agreement. People quickly and easily forget.

Try this sometime: Ask people if they ever saw a visual aid that you showed on a previous call. Often they will have no recollection of having seen it before. Whatever you do, don't make an issue of the fact that they saw it before. Accept the reality of human forgetfulness and deliver that part of your presentation just as though it were to a new prospect.

Likewise, on a return visit, when you previously got an agreement from a prospect as to a need, begin your presentation with something like this:

"As you may recall from my last visit, you said. . . ." Then restate the essence of the agreement and end with, "Isn't that right?"

Here is how Tim Wall might have begun the dialog on his return visit with the dairy farmer.

"As you may recall from my last visit, you said it was important for you to figure out a way to cut down on some of your chores and still produce the same amount of milk. Isn't that right?"

A Misuse of Paraphrasing

There is no good reason to paraphrase facts. Consider this pointless dialog Tim Wall might have had with the dairy farmer:

Tim:	When was that silo built?
Farmer:	1951.
Tim:	So it's about forty years old, isn't that right?
Farmer:	About that.
Tim:	How many cows are you milking?
Farmer:	Forty-eight.
Tim:	Close to half a hundred, huh?
Farmer:	Pretty close.
Tim:	Do you have any help on this operation?
Farmer:	No.
Tim:	I gather, then, that you work it all by yourself, right?
Farmer:	You got it right.

That kind of conversation is likely to cause irritation. The rule is *paraphrase needs, not facts.*

Here is a recap of what usually takes place in a sales opener using a paraphrase:

1. Give your opening statement.
2. Prospect responds with indifference.
3. Probe for a need. Listen carefully for unexpressed meanings and feelings.
4. Prospect makes a vague statement that hints at or attempts to cover up a need.
5. Paraphrase the prospect's vague statement by rephrasing it into a more specific expression which clarifies the need. Use lead-in phrases such as:
   "What I hear you saying is . . ."
   "I take it, though, that . . ."
   "It sounds as if . . ."
   "As I understand it, you mean . . ."
   "Would it be correct to say . . ."
   "It seems to me . . ."
6. An agreement about the need by the prospect is an important conclusion to a paraphrase. To elicit the agreement, end a paraphrase with a closed-end questioning phrase such as:
   ". . . is that what you mean?"
   ". . . wouldn't it?"
   ". . . isn't it?"
   ". . . that's what you really want, isn't it?"
   ". . . aren't you?"
   ". . . isn't that right?"
   ". . . right?"
   ". . . wouldn't you say?"
   When these questions are answered affirmatively, an agreement is being confirmed. It is unlikely that anyone would retract that kind of agreement once it is confirmed.
7. Suggest a benefit your product or service offers that will satisfy the need.
8. Suggest a time for an appointment to make a complete presentation.

And now let's take a look at some examples:

No Time for Distributors

A retail specialty store has been buying stock direct from various manufacturers because the discount given on direct purchases was substantially more than that available from a wholesale distributor. Also, the one time, some years ago, when the owner tried a distributor, he was loaded down with a lot of slow-moving merchandise that eventually had to be sold way below cost. Ever since, he's had no time for distributor reps—that is, until this conversation took place on the telephone.

Brown: Mr. Green, this is Dick Brown of Service Distributing Company.

Green: Hold it. Sorry, but I don't buy from distributors. I don't think we have anything to talk about.

Brown: I'm aware that you buy direct, Mr. Green, but while I have you on the phone, do you mind telling me something?

Green: What is it you want to know?

Brown: What do you do with slow-moving merchandise that's been on the shelf for a long time?

Green: It doesn't happen. I order only what I know will sell.

Brown: What about items that customers return for refund?

Green: Well, if it's defective, I pack it and send it back to the manufacturer for credit.

Brown: I'd guess you place orders to each manufacturer by mail or phone as stock needs replenishing, right?

Green: Yes.

Brown: Mr. Green, how do you currently keep track of your inventory?

Green: Well, I take a complete inventory once a year, a modified inventory once a month, and of course I keep an eye on the shelves every day.

Brown: Doesn't all this take up a lot of your time and your employees' time? I mean the ordering, the packing and unpacking individual shipments to and from different sources, taking inventory and all.

Green: Not actually. Been doing it for years. We're still in business. So I guess it's working OK.

Brown: Do you ever miss a sale because you don't have an item a customer wants?

Green: Uh, well, sure, once in a while I suppose. Doesn't everybody?

Something in the way Mr. Green answered that last question made Dick Brown suspect that "once in a while" was more of a concern than Mr. Green was letting on and that it was probably costing him more than a fair amount in customer retention and profitable sales. This can be construed as an indirect expression of a need and a cue for the following paraphrase to bring it out into the open and get Mr. Green to agree to explore the possibility of doing something about it.

Brown: Mr. Green, I take it, though, that if you had a more complete stock of merchandise so as to cash in on those missed sales, and if you could order daily from one source on a free WATS line and had daily delivery, guaranteed return for full credit of anything unsalable, one-source billing, plus a monthly printout of your inventory with a forecast of future customer trends—all this requiring no work by you or your staff—you'd sure want to know more about it, wouldn't you?

Green: Well, yes, I suppose so.

That last statement by Mr. Green, the answer to the paraphrase question, is the agreement. It's a turning point in Mr. Green's relationship with distributor salespeople. At last he is admitting he wants to know more about optional ways of operating his business. Now it is natural for Brown to follow

this agreement with a summary of benefits and then ask for
an appointment to present the full story.

Brown: Mr. Green, our experience with other stores similar
to yours shows that they are making many additional
sales from special items we stock for them with our
computerized inventory control system. This system assures that you will have on hand all the
merchandise your customers are likely to ask for,
and yet not be overstocked with items that don't
sell. Our computer will help you keep an ongoing
record of your inventory and make sure it maintains
the best balance for your customers' buying patterns. If an item becomes obsolete, we pick it up
and you get credit for it at the current price. The
result of this is an inventory customized for maximum profit for your store, completely free of obso-
lescent, slow-moving, or overstocked merchandise.
All this is with no effort on the part of you or your
staff. I'd be happy to show you many more advantages that you can evaluate in terms of profit to your
business. Can we get together tomorrow morning at
nine o'clock or would one o'clock in the afternoon
be better?

The fact that this example has to do with a distributor/
retailer relationship is not particularly important. A person
like Mr. Green is common in many types of businesses. He
may possess any combination of these characteristics: conser-
vative, skeptical, working harder than necessary, bound to
tradition, creature of habit, basing important decisions on an
isolated past experience, slow to change but having a dimly
perceived yet growing realization that things are changing in
the business and maybe some of these changes deserve a
closer look.

These people need help. They need vendor sales reps who
apply initiative, persistence, and skill in their use of questions
to probe for needs.

Fine-Tuning Your Approach

Notice in the above example how most of the probing sequence had to do with the prospect's world, not the sales rep's. It also contained a good mix of open- and closed-end questions. As long as Mr. Green was answering questions, it was OK to continue questioning until an important need was uncovered. Notice, too, that the first open-end question concerned a suspected key need and that it sustained Mr. Green's interest enough to allow the questioning to continue.

The sales rep didn't uncover Green's strong feelings about the discount differential or the merchandise overload experience. Nor was it necessary to do so in this contact. His objective was to get an appointment to present the full story with Green's mind open. Any objections coming out of those feelings would be better dealt with in person.

Other distributor reps calling on Mr. Green were cherry pickers who turned tail at his habitual initial rebuff, which was grounded in a single experience with a shortsighted distributor of another era.

But the nature and scope of distributor operations is changing. They now provide more sophisticated services. Computers enter the picture. Distributors can afford to purchase them and offer retailers benefits that more than pay for the difference in discount.

Look at the changes in your business. Look for innovations that provide unique benefits for your clientele. Look for tradition-bound prospects who need to be brought up to date, especially those who are quick to discourage your opening remarks. It's a safe bet they are doing that to other salespeople who just as quickly turn away looking for someone more congenial. There is less competition for the time and business of skeptics, which makes them excellent prospects.

A Case Involving Price Resistance

A perennial objection salespeople must deal with is price resistance. But quality costs more. Quality is usually worth the added cost and it takes skilled and determined salespeople to bring the proof to a resisting marketplace.

A salt company manufactures a high-quality salt. When used in processing meat, it markedly improves the flavor and retards spoilage as compared with ordinary salt. Even though this salt costs more, the benefits of improved salability of meat products due to better taste and longer-lasting freshness make it more than worth the added cost.

Salt sales rep Irene Beneski makes an opener to Herman Schmaltz, owner of Schmaltz Meat Company. Schmaltz knows of the salt company Beneski represents. He also knows that its prices are higher than what he is currently paying so he responds to Beneski's opener by muttering, "I'm not interested in buying your high-priced salt." Beneski continues by probing:

Beneski: Mr. Schmaltz, have you read the article in this month's *Meat Packing Journal* regarding the trend away from chemical preservatives in processing meat?

Schmaltz: It seems to me I remember something like that.

Beneski: What did you think of it?

Schmaltz: I'm afraid the end result is consumers are going to be disappointed when they find their meat won't last as long in the refrigerator.

Beneski: Did you also read the article about our HQ salt in that same issue?

Schmaltz: I just glanced through it. But I know one thing. You don't need any kind of fancy salt to cure meat. Good old-fashioned rock salt does just as well and it costs a lot less.

Beneski: It seems to me, though, that if you could establish consumer preference for a brand that stays fresh longer and tastes better, the increased sales volume that would result would be well worth putting out a better-quality product, wouldn't it?

Schmaltz: It might.

Opening a Closed Mind—An Important First Step

Sometimes the prospect's response to a paraphrase is not total agreement. But even, as in this case, "It might" suggests that he would at least be agreeable to hearing more about it. So Beneski continues:

Beneski: Mr. Schmaltz, I can show you some interesting case studies of how other meat packers have increased market share with bacon, sausage, ham, and luncheon meats. The studies show how a consumer panel identified their brands as the ones that not only tasted better but gave them longer storage time as well. Would you have twenty minutes to take a look now?

Real Estate for Sale by Owner

A real estate agent knocks on the door of a home with a sign on the lawn, "For Sale by Owner."

Agent: Are you the owner of this house?

Owner: Yes.

Agent: My name is Beth Jones. I'm a realtor. Do you permit realtors to participate in the sale of your house?

Owner: No.

Agent: Have you talked with other realtors?

Owner: Yes, and I told them what I'm going to tell you. We've decided to try to sell it ourselves. We prefer not to pay the commission.

Agent: I can't blame you for wanting to make as much as you can. How long have you had your house for sale?

Owner: About two months.

Agent: Do you have any idea why it hasn't sold yet?

Owner: I guess houses just aren't moving very fast today.

Agent: How did you happen to arrive at your price?

Owner: We just figured this is about what we'd like to get out of it.

Agent: Have you looked at any competitive market data?

Owner: Well, uh, no.

Agent: Don't you think that might be some important information to have?

Owner: I guess we don't know much about that.

Agent: It sounds as if it could be of help to you if we sat down for a few minutes and discussed this. I'd be happy to share some ideas with you about competitive market data, how prices are determined, and how you can arrange some creative financing that could help you close a sale with someone who would like to buy your house but may have some difficulty arranging financing through ordinary channels. Could we do that now?

Another Busy Prospect Finds the Time

Sam McKay sells employee incentive programs. Here is how he got an appointment with Mr. Glover, a busy personnel vice president at a computer manufacturer.

Glover: Look, I'm sure you have a great idea, but I have a pile of work on my desk . . .

McKay: Mr. Glover, I don't underestimate your workload for a minute. You're responsible for benefits and compensation for the whole company, aren't you?

Glover: That's right.

McKay: And top management is pretty concerned about rising personnel costs when productivity isn't rising too?

Glover: You expect me to answer that question?

McKay: But that just makes your job harder because it means you have to justify every decision, right?

Glover: That's what I get paid for.

McKay: Do you have time to follow the literature on incentive programs at high-tech companies like yours?

Glover: I don't even have time to get my oil changed.

McKay: Well, a recent article pointed out that in high-tech companies the cost of recruitment and on-the-job training is about a third higher than in other industries. They said that turnover was the biggest nightmare. How do you feel about that?

Glover: I don't need to read trade magazines to tell me that.

Here Comes the Paraphrase

McKay: I guess what you're saying is that turnover really adds to your workload. Is that right?

Glover: That's the real problem.

McKay: Mr. Glover, our high-tech clients tell us that our incentive programs have helped to substantially reduce turnover. You could get a pretty good idea if it would be worth considering for your company in just twenty to thirty minutes. Could we do that Wednesday, or would Thursday morning be more convenient for you?

Glover: Uh, Wednesday. Yes, that would be better, but I better check my book.

Some readers may think that Sam was a little too persistent with a harried executive. But Sam's persistence was tempered by the fact that until the need for Sam's program was identified, everything Sam said was about Mr. Glover's world, not Sam's, about Mr. Glover's problems, not Sam's. Also, everything Sam said was a question. Remember those two important keys to persistence. The bottom line is that Sam did Mr. Glover a favor by hanging in there to get him to consider a solution to a critical problem he was struggling with. On the other hand, Sam would have been remiss in copping out when a need for his program was suspected.

In this area of downsizing in companies, executives like Mr. Glover are often harried, taking over tasks that were previously shared with others now departed. If salespeople are reluctant to apply reasonable, judicious persistence with these busy people, many important needs will go unmet. People in business typically wear blinders. The blinders keep them focused on problems immediately before them. The problems are often brush fires that could have been avoided by taking the time to consider preventative measures.

Enter a salesperson with experience in preventative methods others have used in similar circumstances, willing to share his or her time and expertise. As professionals, I believe we are guilty of malpractice when we neglect to use whatever verbal skills we have at our command to help the harried ones in the marketplace to become aware of needs they otherwise fail to see.

What to Do When the Need Is Stated

Jean Serpi sells dishwashing soap to the restaurant trade. She is on the phone to arrange an appointment with G. C. King, a hard-to-see purchasing agent for a large restaurant chain. Jean made the mistake of not leading with a benefit, and was almost rebuffed, but wisely did some probing to recover:

Serpi: Mr. King, my name is Jean Serpi with Dynamo Products. Did you have a chance to read the letter I sent you regarding our new low-temp dishwashing detergent?

King: No, I guess I didn't. Dishwashing soap isn't high on my list of concerns. We did a comprehensive value analysis on soap so we're sure we're getting the best product for our money.

Serpi: Tell me this, Mr. King, where does the cost of energy rate on your list of concerns?

King: That rates pretty high. Actually my biggest concern today is cutting costs. Energy costs, for one, are getting out of hand. Now if you had something in competition with the gas or electric company, I'd be willing to listen. But soap, no. We're getting the best bang for our buck with soap.

Serpi: Actually, Mr. King, the purpose of my call is to arrange an appointment with you to show how our low-temperature dishwashing program can appreciably lower your energy costs. For our customers with restaurants averaging $50,000 in food sales per month, our low-temp-program average energy saving is between $1,500 and $1,800 per year. I'd be happy to show you how it works. I have some open spots on my schedule Thursday. Would morning or afternoon be better for you?

In this example the prospect brought the need out into the open himself. There is no reason to use a paraphrase here. The prospect is looking for a solution to a problem he is well aware of. So all Jean Serpi had to do was to state a benefit that offered a solution to the problem and ask for an appointment.

Try Your Hand at Paraphrasing

Paraphrase the following statements. Start out with a lead-in phrase from item 5 on page 155. Follow your paraphrase with an ending phrase from item 6. The ending phrase is important because when the prospect answers affirmatively, it is agreed that what you said is what was meant even though it wasn't said at first.

1. "I tried to read that book, couldn't keep my mind on it, and finally fell asleep."

2. "Oh boy, this is one time I'm especially glad to see Friday afternoon roll around."
3. Suppose you sell advertising. You are calling on a retail merchant who says, "Business is terrible. We just have to cut back on spending money."

SUGGESTED PARAPHRASES

1. "I take it that the book was boring, wasn't it?"
2. "Sounds as if you had a rough week, right?"
3. "It seems to me you need more store traffic that will get your cash registers buzzing. And that's what you really want, isn't it?"

In a paraphrase avoid direct mention of the product or service you sell. Remember the basic principles covered in Chapters 5 and 6. Talk about what it does, not what it is. In other words you wouldn't say, "It seems to me you need more advertising, don't you?"

How to Become an Expert Paraphraser

The technique of paraphrasing is so valuable you will benefit much from reading this chapter several times until you can effortlessly proceed with a paraphrase whenever you hear hints of needs or cover-ups. As you reread this chapter, recall the times prospects rebuffed your opening remarks and you had good reason to believe they had needs you could satisfy. Perhaps they were only vaguely aware or even totally unaware of their needs.

If possible discuss these situations with other salespeople in your business. Do some creative brainstorming. Practice role-playing these situations with each other. Record these role-play sessions on a tape recorder and critique the playback.

Above all, in the real world of selling, be alert to use paraphrases when you hear vague generalities that hint of possible needs or you hear outright cover-ups.

An important key to applying tactful and effective persistence that will help you get business that many other salespeople miss is to understand this dimension. People buy because of their needs, wants, problems, and dissatisfactions. Often they are not aware of their needs. Sometimes when they do perceive a need, they are still reluctant to take action. It is an important task of the sales profession to bring these needs into perspective, to guide clientele along a path of making intelligent decisions that will benefit them.

Paraphrasing is a preeminent technique to help you do just that.

Chapter 11

GETTING THROUGH TO THE BUYING AUTHORITY

Before P. T. Barnum went on the road with "The Greatest Show on Earth," he had already made a fortune with his American Museum in New York City. The museum became such a great attraction, patrons would bring their lunches and stay all day. Every day thousands would be lined up waiting to get in and spend their money, but they couldn't because the place had limited capacity and the crowd was not turning over fast enough.

So Barnum had a fancy, inviting passageway built. Above it a huge sign announced THIS WAY TO THE EGRESS. A continuous procession of curious people would walk through this passageway expecting to see another wonder of the world. As they walked through a door at the end of the tunnel, they found themselves out in an alley unable to get back in without paying another admission. There were always plenty at the front door eager to take their place. At least they added another word to their vocabularies when they found out that *egress* meant *exit*.

Beware of the Egress

Does this story have anything to do with selling? It sure does! When you know the person you are calling on has the authority to buy yet fobs you off on someone who lacks authority, look out! It could be the way to the "egress." If you go for it too quickly, you are apt to find yourself on the outside with no sale. Or worse, the lower authority will have you believing he or she is doing a selling job on the inside for you. But it would not be reasonable to expect that person to do the kind of selling job you are experienced in doing. Besides, a lot of high-priority time can be invested in callbacks that end up nowhere.

Observing my clients' salespeople in action in the field and in discussing this matter with sales executives, I find that a common error of salespeople is to fail to make a persistent effort in convincing the right buying authority to agree to a sales interview. And conversely they tend to be too quick and eager to spend time with persons in the prospect organization who can say no but do not have the authority to say yes.

I don't mean to say you should slight or risk offending subordinates. There will be times when you will have no choice but to open and even present to them. And when you do, give them your best effort. Give them every courtesy you would give to Number One. Sometimes they have important influence in the final decision. There are situations in which several people at various levels in the organizational hierarchy are involved in the decision. By all means cultivate them with care. In such cases you probably know that it is necessary to sell in depth and you do it with planned intent.

But too often salespeople will carelessly or unwittingly allow themselves to be confronted with the persons who can't make a positive decision. And so they end up with no more than frustration to show for their efforts.

When to Set the Stage

The critical time in setting up sales presentations on the right basis with the proper buying authority is at the very first approach.

I happen to be a great believer in odds. There is a neat, predictable, mathematical precision to them. The multibillion-dollar insurance industry thrives on them. So do Las Vegas and Atlantic City.

Unless you are sure a lower-level employee has the authority to make a buying decision for what you are selling, be aware that opening to that person is to proceed at great risk.

Even under the most favorable circumstances, you can sell only a certain percentage of your prospects. Anything that affects those circumstances less favorably will also diminish your odds of making a sale. To make your objective anyone below the decision-making level has a serious diminishing effect on your odds. A batter in baseball can swing at pitches outside the strike zone and get a hit occasionally. But with every such swing, the batting average goes down.

Every time you make a call it's like stepping into the batter's box. Every time you open to the right person, you are taking a level swing at a ball that is in the strike zone. When you open to someone who can't make the decision you are going for a pitch outside the strike zone. You may, on occasion, make a sale starting out this way, but your ratio of sales to calls will go down. The net result will be precious selling time wasted and lower total sales volume.

If you agree that time is money—that in the sales profession you translate time into revenue for your company and into personal income—then the gambling tables of Las Vegas or Atlantic City would give you better odds for your money than you get from the monetary value of the time spent with the wrong person in a selling situation.

Identify and Approach the Decision Maker First

Even in cases where you know in advance that several people are likely to be involved in a buying decision, make every effort to first approach the person with the highest decision-making authority. This doesn't necessarily mean it's the chief executive officer, although sometimes it is. Rather, it is the person in the highest position in the organization who is directly involved in making purchasing decisions for whatever you sell. There are several advantages for making this person the objective of your first contact.

In the first place, this right person may agree to a complete interview. This is more likely to happen if you are skilled in using an effective opener. So now you are right where you should be: in the most advantageous position.

Second, Number One may introduce you to the lower-level person or persons, giving them instructions to hear your story. In this case, you will get preferential treatment and a higher degree of attention and interest than you would by starting at the lower levels.

Third, Number One may tell you just how much authority lower-level persons have, may even tell you that they can buy if they see fit. Whether they can or not, you will know exactly where you stand and be in a better position to figure out how to proceed.

Fourth, Number One may promise to listen to your complete presentation if someone at a lower level likes it but can't buy. It will require a second presentation on your part, but you are a lot better off than starting low and not being able to present directly to the decision maker. For once you start at a lower level, you are stuck at that level. Sometimes subordinates won't admit that they don't have authority to make a final decision. Their ego may get in the way. You could be getting nowhere making repeat calls on such a person. Finally you conclude that you are not at a decision-making level and you are at an impasse. To go over the subordinate's head now is likely to offend this person whom you need to keep on your side.

The alternative is to have the lower-level people do the selling for you up the ladder. Unfortunately, it would be impossible to train them to do anywhere near the kind of selling job you were trained to do. Besides, subordinates don't like to recommend spending money, nor do they like to take the responsibility for approving or requesting something that they could be criticized for later.

Remember Captain Miles Standish. He performed many brave deeds as leader of Plymouth Colony. But when he fell in love with Priscilla Mullens, he sent John Alden to propose to her for him because he didn't have the nerve to do it himself. He lost her as a result of his lack of assertiveness. Likewise, you can lose sales by depending on a go-between.

Therefore it is important to do everything in your power to reserve your initial opener in a prospective organization for the highest-level person involved in making a decision for what you sell. Even though you may get shunted down to a lower level, you have met the top person, who suggested you see someone else. Now if you get nowhere, you have a right to go back to where you began to find out what is going on.

An important point is this: When you do spend time with lower-level influentials, especially when you make an opener to them, be sure that it is necessary or to your advantage and that it is done with your intent.

On the other hand, be sure you are not doing it because it seems easier or is less risk to your ego or because your opening technique is faulty. And never do it without making a carefully planned effort to avoid an impasse.

Effective opening strategy, then, begins with identifying the key decision maker.

Selling to individual consumers does not present any identification difficulty. With a small company it is usually the owner or partners, except for routine purchases that may be delegated to an employee. For example, an office manager buys office supplies, but the boss makes decisions on big-ticket items. A major purchase by homeowners may require the presence of both wife and husband. Make sure appointments are made to include all decision makers in a complete presentation even though the opener may be made to only one.

Who Rules the Roost?

But who is the key decision maker in a small business or in a family?

Irene Reinke sells home improvements. During the warm-up part of her presentation, while she is arranging some of her visual material and samples, Irene asks a question unrelated to her business such as, "Where do you folks like to spend your vacation?" She does not look directly at the couple as she asks it, but instead busies herself with her props. Her reasoning is that she doesn't want to influence one or the other by indicating with her eyes who should answer. She then makes a special attempt to draw out the preferences—and nail down agreements from the first that answers.

How to Approach Large Organizations

In the world of larger business firms and nonprofit institutions, we find a more complex hierarchy of decision-making influentials, with varying degrees of authority and varying degrees of isolation from unsolicited contact by salespeople.

There are no universal rules that apply to every kind of selling situation. Therefore the uniqueness of any particular one must be taken into account in customizing your approach.

Who Is Your Right Person?

Right persons have many different titles depending on what you are selling. Your experience, combined with the experience of other salespeople in your business, has probably sorted out the levels of buying influence to some extent.

If purchasing agents routinely make buying decisions for your product, they are easy to identify. But often P.A.s merely place orders for decisions made elsewhere in that company. Often, too, they won't tell you that. They may lead you to believe you are calling on the right person when they are in fact serving as screens protecting the real decision makers from spending time with salespeople. It is wise to do some sleuthing to find out if this is true before you go over the head of a P.A. Because if a P.A. is, in fact, the real decision maker, you must proceed very cautiously in making other contacts in that organization. Otherwise you can quickly wear out your welcome. Sometimes it's not easy to get the truth regarding who the key influences are. It is such challenges that make selling such an interesting profession.

Authority and responsibilities, regardless of title, vary widely from one organization to another, making it expedient to do some preliminary information gathering. This is true whether or not your prospective organization has purchasing agents.

Your best bet for gathering such information is to develop a nose for this sort of thing. Keep your antennas out, your eyes and ears open to relevant bits and pieces of information. Some salespeople are naturally curious and observant. This comes easily to them. Others need to work at it harder.

I hope that reading Chapters 8 and 9 on questioning and listening techniques has helped to broaden your skill in this area of perceptivity and I hope you practice using these skills. Get in the habit of asking questions of receptionists, other employees of your prospects' organizations, neighbors of the prospects, other salespeople who call on them, or anybody who can shed some light on how buying decisions are made in that organization.

Sources of Right-Person Information

The business section of local newspapers, as well as state and large city business journals, are full of articles about who is who in the business world. Especially scan the columns about people being promoted or changing jobs. Look for articles about new businesses getting started, moving into the area, or expanding.

Networking is a popular form of business-related socializing today. Most large cities have sponsored after-hours networking get-togethers. These provide opportunities for people of related interests to become acquainted and share information. Seek out and attend these sessions.

If you sell to specific industries, become active in associations related to those industries. Read their publications.

Attend their meetings and conventions when possible. In addition to meeting many people who can give you valuable information, you will become directly acquainted with key decision makers. Many national associations have local or regional chapters, making it convenient for you to attend local functions. Better yet, become actively involved. Volunteer for committee assignments. Run for a board of directors seat. Write articles for their publications. Offer to present a program at one of their meetings or educational sessions. You have valuable ideas to share based on your experience serving that industry. In addition to getting vital information, you will accelerate your positioning within the industry.

When making in-person calls, you will spend some time waiting in reception lobbies. These rooms usually have magazines available for your reading pleasure to ease your waiting. They often have annual reports and other literature such as brochures and in-house publications loaded with information you can use. Look for those. You will also see other salespeople sitting there. Strike up an acquaintance with them. Don't be bashful about this. Some of them may have been calling on this account before and are willing to share who's who information with you.

One of the best sources of who's who information is the prospect company's salespeople. They are easy to reach because they return phone calls. They understand your situation and are usually empathetic.

A universal source of right-person information is the central switchboard of your target organization. Ask this question of whomever answers, "Who is the person responsible for decisions regarding [*name your product or service*]?" You will be given a name. Most often receptionists are instructed to give names of lower-level screeners. So then ask, "Whom does that person report to?" The answer will be closer to the true decision maker. Notice the word *decisions* is suggested rather than *purchasing*.

Often titles are an indication of buying authority. But be aware that titles can mean different things in different organizations. A chief executive officer can come with a variety of titles such as president, chairman of the board, vice chairman of the board, chairman of the executive committee, executive vice president, general manager, or simply, manager. Top marketing people could be vice president of marketing, vice president of sales, marketing manager, general sales manager, sales manager, product manager, and so on. Almost all positions have similarly ambiguous titles.

The directories and services listed in Chapter 4 are a good source of identifying the names of people by their titles. If your company doesn't subscribe to any of those services, they can be found in most public libraries. Reference desk librarians are generally glad to help you.

Information in directories tends to be at least a year old from the time they were compiled. Considering today's trend of people changing jobs more often, you may find some of the information out of date. But even if you use the name of the person who formerly held a particular title, it's a simple matter to ask who is the replacement. At least you sound as though you know something about that organization.

Evaluate Information-Gathering Time

As valuable as this information may be, be careful not to spend an inordinate amount of time gathering it. Remember the time clock syndrome, the tendency to view a job as a block of time to be filled with activities. Some salespeople will try to justify doing something other than facing the moment of truth—which is to be in direct contact with prospects and risk rejection, risk failure.

Another factor related to the time clock syndrome is the willingness to spend time with people having lower-level buying authority because they are easier to get in to see and are less likely to cause rejection.

Why Persistence With the Right Person Pays

While it is true that occasionally sales are lost because lower-level people are offended by a salesperson's persistent effort to reach a top decision maker, many more are lost because of futile effort with people who can't buy. Your odds are in favor of persistent effort to reach the top.

So when you are in contact with the right buying authority don't be too quick to accept what I call a *brushdown* to a lower level. You have the attention of the person who is privy to information lower levels may not have. Here is an opportunity to find out how decisions are made, who the decision makers are, and what their criteria are. In other words, you can find out what ground rules you will face.

How to Stay With the Decision Maker

The key to getting high-level decision makers to grant you an interview is to *sell* them on granting you an interview. How do you sell anybody on anything? Go back to the basics. That is, benefits—answers to the question, "What's in it for them?" The emphasis now should be placed on benefits from getting information vital to their organization directly from you, rather than secondhand from a subordinate.

Your manner is more of a determining factor than the words you use. Do you look and sound like a professional who is loaded with ideas, relevant information, and other people's experience you are in a position to share? If there is any interest at all in your information, the decision makers will have questions. Wouldn't it be better for them to get that information directly from you firsthand, rather than from a subordinate? Your presentation may contain some valuable data that Number One could profit from learning firsthand. Getting it firsthand, it would be more complete, would avoid any omissions or distortions in transit, and would save time for everybody concerned.

Perhaps it is important that Number One is in the unique position to evaluate your proposal in terms of the overall operation. Or Number One is the person who can make an immediate decision and so avoid any delay in realizing benefits to the organization. Think of any other benefits unique to your product or service that can be emphasized here.

How to Deal With a Brushdown

Let's say the top decision maker's name is Ms. Wunn and she tries to brush you down to a lower level. Try this tack:

Ms. Wunn: You don't want to see me; you want to see George Fleming. He handles that.

You: Fine. If Mr. Fleming likes it and believes it's right for your firm, can he make the decision to buy it?

How Ms. Wunn answers this question is even more significant than what is said. If the answer is yes, without any hesitation—with a firm, positive ring of certainty to it—Mr. Fleming is probably the right person.

If there is hesitation, any hedging, any elusiveness, anything in the way the reply sounds that gives you reason to doubt that Fleming is the decision maker, he probably isn't. Then you will be wise to do some further probing. Specifically, ask if Fleming would report back to Ms. Wunn with a briefing and if the decision would then be made jointly.

But if the answer to your first question is no, you know who is really going to make the decision. You can also be pretty sure that the selling job Fleming makes to the decision maker will be nowhere near as complete and effective as yours would be.

Other valuable information can be gained from Ms. Wunn such as when purchases are likely to be made, what the organization has done in the past, whether there is any competition lurking in the wings, what the organization likes or doesn't like about past experience or competitive products, what else is in the hopper, what obstacles there may be to your getting an order. Be sure to include open-end questions to get at feelings and attitudes that affect buying decisions. This kind of priceless information is more likely to be divulged at a higher level than by a subordinate who may not be certain about what is or is not confidential and may fear being held responsible for leaking information that shouldn't be freely given.

Besides, the added dialog may present an opportunity to convince Ms. Wunn to take a firsthand look after all or be included in the interview with Fleming.

When a Subordinate Can Make a Decision

Suppose Ms. Wunn convinces you that George Fleming has authority to make a decision. If it is an in-person call, ask Ms. Wunn to introduce you to Mr. Fleming. Often in similar situations, a Ms. Wunn would take me down the hall to a Mr. Fleming's office and say, "George, here's someone with an idea that I'd like you to take a look at." At this point I have at least rounded first base and am still running.

If your opener to Ms. Wunn was made on the phone, the introduction could be made from a three-way conversation. But Ms. Wunn is not likely to do that unless you ask her. Even if Ms. Wunn doesn't introduce you to Mr. Fleming, she could tell Fleming to be expecting your call. Even if she doesn't do that, when you make your opener to Fleming, you can say, ". . . Ms. Wunn asked me to call you to arrange an appointment for a time at your convenience when you could evaluate an idea that. . . ." Wouldn't you consider that a pretty strong referral?

How a Master Gets the Right Person

Tony Pernelli sells employee motivation programs. He makes his first opener to the president of prospective companies. Often the president will tell him that the personnel manager is the one he should see. But Tony knows from experience that personnel managers almost never have a budget for his type of program. The final approval usually has to come from the president. I watched Tony in action as he called on S. A. Amundson, the president of a medium-size manufacturing company. Here's how Tony got Mr. A. to hear him out.

Mr. A.: The person you should be talking to is Bert Dierks, the personnel manager. Employee motivation is his area of concern.

Tony: Well, Mr. Amundson, certainly Mr. Dierks should sit in with us, as I'm sure we could profit from his thinking. But, Mr. Amundson, I deliberately came to see you for three very good reasons. The first is, you, more than anyone else in your organization, are vitally interested in evaluating the cost-cutting effect my program can have on your P&L statement. Second, you are the one person here who could honestly be called unprejudiced toward a particular department, since you alone can see the whole operation, or the big picture. And that puts you in the best possible position to know almost immediately whether or not what I have can help you cut costs. And third, Mr. Amundson [at this point Tony has a big smile on his face], you are the one person in the organization who can make an immediate decision and we both know how expensive procrastination can be.

With this technique, you must use language that is relevant to the person to whom you are talking. In this case Tony's decision maker is a chief executive officer. A primary concern of a CEO of most companies is the profit and loss statement. Ordinarily, no one else has as much responsibility to that piece of paper. So when Tony referred to it, Mr. Amundson had to agree that he, more than anyone else in the company, held that vital interest.

Mr. Amundson also knew that his evaluation, uniquely, would be unprejudiced toward a particular department. For example, a sales manager would want to buy something that would make the sales department look good. A manufacturing manager would agree to anything that made the manufacturing department look good. Every department head would welcome and encourage any extra budgetary item that favored his niche. But the CEO has a better view of the overall company welfare.

Tony's third point touches upon a common trait in many of us. We like to be nice persons. We don't like to give anyone a flat-out no. This is especially true of CEOs. They instinctively practice good public relations. Many came up the ranks through sales, so they have a fair amount of empathy toward salespeople. In the back of their mind, they may doubt if they would make a change the sales rep suggests. So instead of a no, they fob us off to a subordinate. Now we're out of sight, out of mind. A salesperson less perceptive than Tony would tend to go quickly for the egress, hoping where no hope exists.

I would rather get a no today than a no next month. And I would rather get it from a person that calls the shots so I know exactly where I stand. Wouldn't you?

Keep the Right Door Open

Now suppose Ms. Wunn told you that George Fleming can't make a buying decision and you tried Tony Pernelli's technique. Ms. Wunn responded with, "Look, I don't have time to visit with every salesperson that calls on us. I delegate these things to Fleming. If you want to do business us you have to talk to Fleming and that's it."

Then try this:

Of course, I will discuss this with anyone in your organization you want me to. But if Mr. Fleming likes it and believes it's right for your firm, would the door be open for me to come back and present it to you firsthand?

You will, of course, play the game according to Ms. Wunn's rule, but you have every right to negotiate to play the game by your rule. Remember what was said in Chapter 2. Your business is just as legitimate as the businesses of the people you call on. Your time is just as valuable as their time. You are equals. Do you believe that?

Your rule is: If Mr. Fleming determines that what you have to offer will benefit the company, but Fleming can't make a buying decision, then in all fairness, the person who can make the decision, who asked you to spend your valuable time with Mr. Fleming, ought to consider the proposal firsthand. Do you agree?

If Ms. Wunn agrees to your request to come back and present it to her personally, it will take two separate presentations, but you are on fairly solid ground going to Fleming. However, if the answer is no, realize that your odds have fallen considerably.

Making a Judgment Call

Now you have to make a judgment call. Judgment is difficult to teach. It comes from a combination of experience and intuition. However, the criteria for making a judgment call are based on answers to questions such as:

- How good is the potential of business from Ms. Wunn's company?
- Does the company have an obvious or serious problem for which you have a solution?
- Is it the kind of company you prefer to do business with?
- Is the company in the market for what you sell?
- Is there a good possibility that Mr. Fleming's recommendation would be strong enough to get approval from Ms. Wunn?
- Would you be able to get valuable information from Fleming?
- Is there a possibility that your refusal to talk to Fleming will endanger your position for future business?

You may think of other questions that uniquely apply to your situation.

If it is a marginal prospect, if the answers to the above questions are largely negative, if you have better prospects elsewhere, you may be better off elsewhere. In most cases, you are not risking your time on just one call with Mr. Fleming. Too often, a Mr. Fleming will show some interest and you will make repeated callbacks. You may also spend valuable time preparing lengthy, comprehensive proposals. All for naught. Remember this all started with Ms. Wunn giving you the classic brushdown.

There are three little words we concern ourselves with in the sales profession: yes, no, and maybe. The first two we can take to the bank. But the last one can cause grief. At least with a no, we can leave that situation behind and go on to more promising grounds.

I recall working on a consulting assignment with a sales rep who proudly declared to me that he had made sixteen calls on a prospect and *they haven't said no yet*! Of course, in selling certain big-ticket or high-volume products or services, it may require such a number of repeat calls or even more. But the case I'm referring to did not, and that happens all too often. Make wise judgment calls so that your time will be used where it will do the most good for everybody concerned.

Despite your best efforts to reach decision makers, there will be times when you find yourself in the company of subordinates. As was mentioned earlier, sometimes lower-level persons are reluctant to admit they don't have buying authority. You need to find that out. And since their ego may come into play, your questions must be tactful. Instead of asking a blunt question such as, "Do you have authority to make a decision?" Try these:

- "What is the decision-making process?"
- "Is anyone else involved in the decision?"
- "What is your role in the decision-making process?"
- "How were decisions made in the past?"
- "How does the purchasing committee function?"

If it is determined that the boss is the one who really makes the decision, your best bet is to *sell* the idea of getting to the top person by citing the benefits of doing that. Say something like this:

> It's not fair for me to expect you to do the selling for me. May I suggest you set an appointment with your boss for the three of us to get together. This way you will get credit for recommending a good idea and I'll get credit for doing my job of selling. It will save time for all three of us, because I'll be able to share my experience on how this product is used by firms similar to yours and I'll be able to answer any questions either of you may have.

Make it clear that your intent is to help make the best presentation possible. You are offering to co-author it. You add value—your expertise, your experience. The boss could have questions or objections which the subordinate may have difficulty answering, but which are routine for you. You will make him look good.

When using the techniques in this chapter, remember, you are a guest in the domain of one who is accustomed to calling the shots there. Don't let the firmness of your suggestions appear to be a demand. Make it clear that you are stating your terms, but that the decision to grant the interview is entirely in the hands of the prospect. Establish the fact that you are a high-grade individual of equal business stature. Your manner must show that you have full confidence in what you are selling, that you know from previous experience your proposal is valid and will be of benefit to the prospect.

There Are No Absolute Rules

The techniques suggested here are not hard-and-fast rules that apply to every brushdown attempt. In some instances an executive may tell you a subordinate does not have a clear buying mandate and yet that executive will make decisions based on recommendations from below. And in any one instance the right thing for you to do may be to present to the lower-level person.

But remember the matter of odds. They are not in your favor when a lower-level person does not have clear-cut authority. And if you repeatedly accept brushdowns, the law of averages will see to it that in the long run you'll be spinning your wheels, spending precious time presenting to and following up with people who do not have much influence in the buying decision. That time could be more profitably spent looking for a right person somewhere else. Besides, you are better off to avoid the emotional drain that goes with pursuing dead ends.

Most important, realize that you will greatly improve your selling skill and consequent performance when you become more determined to hang in longer with a higher-level buying authority. At least find out the ground rules so you know where you stand. Settling for lower authority may seem like taking the easier road at first, but the road will become more difficult along the way.

Putting It All in Perspective

This chapter states a central theme of cold call selling: Getting a top-level decision maker to hear your presentation firsthand is in itself a sale to be made. The ability to do so is a paramount selling skill. Regardless of the range of your sales experience, you now have this ability to some degree. It is crucial for you to realize the importance of committing yourself to a never-ending quest to improve this skill.

Although the words you use in your dialog with a top authority are important, the quest cannot begin and end with just the words. Remember in Chapter 2, when we considered the subject of self-image, it was said:

You can learn the words, even practice techniques by role-playing with other salespeople in a training session. But the words, phrases, and techniques won't work for you in the real world with a live prospect unless you believe you have every right to an audience with a high-level person. Because if you don't believe you do, you will subconsciously do whatever you have to do to get where you believe you belong.

The complete skill lies in understanding and putting into practice all the principles covered in this book.

Chapter 12

THE GATEKEEPERS

Before you have an opportunity to state your opener to the Number One decision maker, you must first talk to receptionists and secretaries or executive assistants. This chapter contains applications for both in-person calls and telephoning.

Chapter 14 deals with telephone techniques and includes dialog with the gatekeepers. But for now let's concentrate on in-person calls.

In the reception lobby you may find handout brochures with a message telling how welcome salespeople are and that they will be given every opportunity to tell their story. But that may be on the company's terms, which is the lowest level in a screening hierarchy. Receptionists and secretaries are often trained to protect busy executives from avoidable interviews with salespeople who would waste an executive's time.

On the other hand, receptionists and secretaries also are given responsibility to see to it that visitors who have something beneficial to offer their organization will be helped in every way possible to state their case to the company's best advantage.

If your objective is to reach a top executive, you will often find that a receptionist tends to steer you in the direction of a lower-level screener. This type of receptionist may voluntarily do very little to help you get to the top-level buying authority and, if not treated properly, can do a great deal to keep you out.

When I use the term gatekeeper, I think of it in the positive sense that it is someone who is going to open the gate for me to the decision maker.

How to Greet Receptionists

In order to elicit proper treatment, your attitude is important. You are not a time waster; you have ideas, information, experience, and expertise that will be valuable to the right persons in the organization whether they buy from you or not. Your manner is one of unhesitating confidence yet without pretense or cockiness. A big, warm, friendly smile will go a long way toward helping you feel self-confident as well as toward making a good impression with other people.

It seems terribly elementary to mention the importance of smiling to anyone in sales. It is one of those things that should go without saying. Yet the next time you sit in a reception lobby where other salespeople approach a receptionist, watch their faces. How seldom you will see a genuine, warm smile.

With some people a smile comes easily, naturally. Others need to work at it. I had to. I can remember many photos taken when I was sure there was a nice wide grin on my face. But when the prints came back, not so. If you've experienced the same phenomenon, better work on it.

It is best to tell a receptionist as little as possible without being deceptive and without making it obvious you want to tell as little as possible. This may seem contrary to today's trend toward openness. But there are times when it is to everyone's benefit to be less open. This is such a time. You want to avoid having a receptionist prejudge the nature of your call and send you to the wrong person. You want to avoid the wasted time and frustration that is caused by taking such a direction at this stage.

You have a strategy for setting a course of action that will enable you to make the most effective use of everybody's time in serving the needs of prospective clients. You are rendering them a great service in taking pains to set it up right. Receptionists may not understand this. It is not your job to teach them to understand it. Therefore, you have little choice but to maintain a careful balance between reserve and openness. To do otherwise is to risk walking into the passageway that leads to an egress.

To readers who call on buyers who are readily accessible, it may sound like I'm overdoing this business of being extra careful in getting to the right person. These techniques may not be necessary for them. I beg your forbearance and ask you to take from this book what applies to you.

When You Don't Know the Name

When approaching a receptionist, it is helpful to know the name of the person you want to see. But in case you don't know the name, don't let that stop you from making a call. Let's say your objective is to arrange an appointment with the president of a company and you don't know the name. Here is an approach to take:

You:	Good morning. I'd like to speak to the president of your company. Who would that be, please?
Receptionist:	Thomas Jackson.
You:	Would you please tell Mr. Jackson *[your name]* from *[your company]* is here to see him.
Receptionist:	What is this in regard to?
You:	The purpose of my call is to meet Mr. Jackson, state my business, and arrange an appoint-

ment. Would you please tell him that *[your name]* is here to see him.

You have answered the receptionist's question honestly. She asked you the purpose of the call. You told her it was to meet Mr. Jackson, state your business, and arrange an appointment. On the other hand, you haven't given her any information that would allow her to prejudge the nature of your call and send you to someone else.

Rarely will receptionists ask you any questions beyond that. Additional probing is usually beyond their domain. If someone sitting at a receptionist's desk asks you further questions at this point, it's probably not a receptionist, but someone replacing the receptionist who is on break, out to lunch, or out sick.

Sometimes receptionists will say, "Mr. Jackson doesn't see anyone without an appointment." Then simply repeat what you just said, patiently, with a pleasant smile on your face.

Another approach when you do not know the name of the person you want to call on is to ask an unusual question about that person. Let's say this time you want the top financial executive. You don't even know the title. It could be vice president of finance, comptroller, controller, treasurer, manager of accounting, or whatever.

You: I have a question.
Receptionist: OK, what is it?
You: Is your chief financial executive a man or a woman?
Receptionist: A woman.
You: What is her name?
Receptionist: Betty Ross.
You: Would you please tell Ms. Ross that *[your name]* from *[your company]* is here to see her.

The essence of this technique is to ask simple, closed-end questions that are easy for the receptionist to answer. This will help you maintain the initiative, get information you need, and lead you to your objective. In the preceding example you ordinarily wouldn't need to know Ms. Ross's title at this stage. You can find that out later. Avoid asking any more questions than necessary when there is a risk of being sent to a wrong person. When that risk is not present, feel free to get as much information as you can from a receptionist.

When You Do Know the Name

When you know the name of the person you want to see, your approach would be: "Good morning. Would you please tell Ms. Betty Ross that *[your name]* from *[your company]* is here to see her." This has a sound of positive expectancy. Even though you don't have an appointment and you are not saying that you do, this approach will call for higher regard from a receptionist than if you start out with, "Is Betty Ross in?"

These approaches will usually get you directly to the person you want to see or to his or her secretary. Sometimes a question will be relayed to the receptionist, "What is this in regard to?" Don't try to give your opener to be relayed back. Instead say: "The purpose of my call is to meet Ms. Ross, state my business, and arrange an appointment." Sometimes you will get relayed back, "But what is your business?"

Simply ask, "Could I please state it directly to Ms. Ross?"

Keep your response in the form of a simple question. It is unlikely anyone would say no to that. The receptionist may ask you to pick up a lobby phone. Ms. Ross is on the line. Your request for direct contact is being honored. Go ahead now and state your opener over the phone. Don't press for face-to-face contact until after you give your opening benefit.

How to Greet Secretaries

Sometimes Ms. Ross's secretary will either come out to meet you in the lobby or be on the line when you pick up the lobby phone.

Secretaries, or executive assistants as they are often called, usually require different dialog than receptionists. Whereas a receptionist's responsibility is directing calls to everyone in the organization, secretaries are specifically concerned with one or a few individuals. They tend to be more skilled in the art of tactfully keeping unknown quantities out of their boss's office. Unconvinced of the importance of your mission, they will keep you out. On the other hand, when they believe you have something that will benefit their organization, they become invaluable allies. The higher you go in an organizational hierarchy, the smarter and more powerful secretaries will be. Any hint of arrogance, tactlessness, or manipulation on your part is going to hurt your cause.

Secretaries tend to be adept and determined at getting the essential details of why you want to see the boss. The more information they get, the better they are doing their job. Your task is to give them enough information to justify recommending you for an interview. At the same time, avoid giving them any reason to make assumptions about your proposal that could curtail an opportunity to make a sale or get you shunted off to a screener.

Let's go back to the example in which your objective is to arrange an appointment with the president of a company. You get through your dialog with the receptionist. A woman comes out to the reception desk and says, "I am Linda, Mr. Jackson's assistant. What can I do for you?" Continue with:

My name is *[your name]* from *[your company]*. The special reason for my visit here this morning is to meet Mr. Jackson, state my business to him, and arrange an appointment. Could we do that now?

She may usher you into Jackson's office without any special comment. But more likely she will ask a question such as: "What is this in regard to?" Your reply should be something like this:

We are working with many firms similar to yours, with an idea that our clients tell us substantially cuts their operating costs [*or whatever general benefit applies to what you sell*]. In my experience I have found that the president can quickly determine whether or not your company would want to consider this idea. Could I meet him now?

This is the time to use general rather than specific benefits. And since it is the president of the company you want to speak with, use words that reflect a broad area of concern that is the domain of a president such as *operating cost* or *operational policy*. If instead, you were to use the words *cut manufacturing costs,* Linda would probably direct you to someone in manufacturing. That person may eventually turn out to be the right one, but you don't know that yet. At this point, your objective by an earlier decision is the president. (However, should your objective be someone other than the president, substitute that title for *president* in the preceding script.)

When there is a reason for urgency to your request for an immediate contact, be sure to emphasize it. There may be a limited offer or an impending price change. When you are working out of town, mention where you are from and the fact that now, while you are here, is the best, maybe the only, opportunity for your prospect to learn about your idea. This is not the same as saying, "I just happened to be in the neighborhood."

Especially in larger organizations, executive secretaries can have a great deal of clout. Sometimes they know almost as much about what is going on as the boss does. You want to be very careful to avoid offending such people. They are particularly skilled at getting all the information they want, so when a secretary presses for more information, take this tack:

I appreciate your question, but I have no way of telling you all about it in just a few words. If you prefer, I'd be happy to arrange a time at your convenience and go over the details with you.

This will qualify her. Because if she doesn't have clout, she's not likely to make the appointment with you. Then you can go right back to asking when you can see the boss. But if she does have the clout, you have avoided offending her. If she makes an appointment with you, treat her as though she were the Number One.

Secretaries and Referrals

Here is an approach to a secretary using a referral. After your introduction say:

> My special reason for calling on Mr. Jackson is at the suggestion of one of his business associates who is a customer of ours. He felt certain Mr. Jackson would find a profitable application to a unique idea we've developed. Would you please tell Mr. Jackson that I'm here.

Notice that the referrer's name was not given. Omitting the name here adds an extra touch to arouse Mr. Jackson's curiosity. Besides, the name is not likely to mean anything to the secretary.

And yes, get on a first-name basis with secretaries—and receptionists—as quickly as possible. They are less likely to be offended when called by first name than an executive. A point was made in Chapter 6 that people love to hear the sound of their name. You can be sure this includes gatekeepers. Do whatever fits your natural social style to establish rapport and to nurture the relationship. This is especially beneficial when you make repeated contact with them because the decision maker is unavailable whenever you call.

Avoiding Prejudgment

On the basis of comments from my seminar attendees, some salespeople have misgivings about using the word *idea*, along with a benefit statement, instead of identifying the product or service being sold. But the alternative is prejudgment—a cold call's greatest nemesis.

A secretary asks the question, "What is this in regard to?" because she wants to put a convenient one- or two-word label on the reason for your call. She will take your carefully planned benefit statement and reduce it to what it is, instead of what it will do for the prospect. She will tell the boss that someone is here to sell insurance, investments, advertising, printing, banking, copiers, office leasing, or whatever it is you sell. The boss immediately decides they don't need that. So now where are you? Is this a viable alternative to the benefit idea?

Another possibility is that an assistant will refer you to someone other than the person who was your primary objective. Before you accept that invitation, do some preliminary probing with the assistant to find out just how buying decisions are made in the organization.

The one you're being referred to may be the right person after all. Or if not, give yourself a chance to decide whether or not you are about to walk into an egress, what your odds are, and what course you may want to take. If it's a now-or-never situation, you may decide to go for it. If it's not urgent, another day, another approach may put you on more solid ground.

If you have any reservations about using a benefit statement in your opening remarks either to a secretary or directly to the decision maker, consider this: Selling is a process of negotiation. I have yet to have anyone disagree with that statement. In any negotiation, do you believe it is wise to lay all of your cards on the table face up? Of course not. But that's what happens when you put a label on what you sell. Remember the fundamental concept: People don't buy a product or a service for what it is; they buy for what it will do for them.

Heed Your Style

Another reality we must face is that in all forms of human relations, and especially in selling, it is impossible to please everyone at all times. My friend and fellow sales trainer Hank Trisler says in his book, *No Bull Selling:* "The secret of failure is to try to please everybody. When you try to please everybody, you end up pleasing nobody. Most important of all, you end up not pleasing you, and selling stops being fun."

We want to be liked by others. And we certainly don't want to offend anybody. But it's a fact of life when making cold calls, especially in the business world, we are going to interrupt people who are busy doing other things. This conflicts with our wanting to be nice.

When I make calls with my clients' salespeople, they occasionally approach prospects timidly, tentatively. Then they explain their failure to get an appointment by saying, "You can't be too pushy with these people."

But timidity and pushiness are two extremes of a spectrum with many positive alternatives in between:

Timid   Pushy

A posture that is too near either end of the spectrum will fail equally in attempts to reach decision makers.

The closer you move to the extreme right, the more you risk offending someone. The more you move to the left, the more you risk failure to reach your objective due to prejudgment or being perceived as a time waster.

Where is the right place for you to be on the scale? I can't tell you. Some salespeople can succeed with more assertiveness than others. They may have personality traits that compensate for behavior that in others would be considered to be abrasive.

Where is your comfort zone on the scale? If it's too far to the left, you may need to step out of it in order to reach high-level, well-protected decision makers. Some prospects will tolerate more assertiveness from salespeople than others. How good are you at sensing their assertiveness threshold? No matter how good you are at reading it, there will be times when you read it wrong.

Realizing that I don't always get to the person I want to

reach, I constantly strive to maintain a position on the scale that keeps the odds in my favor.

There will be times when receptionists or secretaries are new on the job. Or things aren't going too well that day, or for some reason they feel anxious and emotionally vulnerable. Be alert to these signs. Concentrate your first effort on helping them feel at ease.

Franklin Delano Roosevelt once said, "Everybody on earth is shy, self-conscious, and unsure of themselves. Everybody is timid about meeting strangers. So if you will just spend the first minute you are in the presence of strangers helping them feel comfortable, you will never suffer from self-consciousness again."

There is an often-told but beautiful line attributed to an old Indian woman who once said, "I like me best when I'm with you." Help people to like themselves. Put them at ease with you. Forget about yourself and any self-conscious feeling you may have. Concentrate on the other person's feelings. He or she will be grateful and return your considerateness. Then you will feel much more self-confident.

And that's exactly the way you want to feel. A poised, confident manner that radiates complete belief in the words being said to the host organization regarding benefits will be the single most important factor in getting the right door opened. Consider that here is the ever-present question in a secretary's mind: "Is this stranger going to be a pestering time waster for the boss or a bearer of important information we can't afford to miss?"

Have an Ally, Not a Buffer

Know that secretaries are dedicated to the welfare of their bosses. They know the moods, whims, preferences, urgencies, and timing that will have an important bearing on the reception you will eventually get from your intended prospect. They quickly sense whether they are being regarded as an obstacle or an ally and will reflect your attitude toward them.

If you see a buffer, if you show impatience or irritation

with the question, "What is this in regard to?" you're going
to get a buffer who calls the shots at this stage and who knows
how to give you a brushoff with ease. The same is true if you
come on cocky, standoffish, patronizing, or overbearing, or if
you come on wishy-washy, indecisive, weasel-worded, or
overanxious.

But if you see an ally who is more concerned than you are
to see that the boss gets important information, and if you
treat this ally with all the courtesy, dignity, and unaffected
warmth that a good ally deserves, a good ally is what you will
get.

The Inevitable Waiting

Cooling the heels in a reception lobby is an unavoidable
way of life for most sales reps calling on business organizations. The perennial question is, "How long should you
wait?" Some claim nice, easy answers to that and say, "Never
wait for longer than fifteen or twenty minutes," or whatever
specific limit they choose to set. That may be all right for a
general rule but some variables dictate that flexibility is wiser.

It is one thing when you have paid hundreds of dollars and
hours of time traveling to get to a key, target prospect, or
when you have word that the prospect is in the process of
making a buying decision on what you sell. It is quite another
when the call is in an area you frequent and there is no reason
to believe a critical purchasing decision is imminent. Good
judgment is the best rule.

When you are in a waiting situation, don't get yourself too
comfortable in a deep-piled reception room chair engrossed
in your favorite magazine. Rather, get into the habit of knowing what is going on at the reception desk without making a
pest of yourself. All too many callers have missed opportunities to see a buyer because a receptionist was under the
pressure of handling more messages than was humanly possible, was distracted, misplaced a note, or was careless, or

because there was a changing of the guard. Realize, too, that receptionists, mortals that they are, are prone to all such misadventures in the pressure-cooker atmosphere of the reception room. Be understanding of the times when it is happening, yet tactfully inquire of the progress being made with your mission. You have every right to know.

Chapter 13

FINE-TUNING YOUR APPROACH

The best opener is a planned opener. The unspoken question in the prospect's mind as you approach is, "Do I want to talk to this salesperson or not?" You need the best answer you can give. It's not likely that the best answer you can give will come spontaneously. There isn't a lot of time for prospects to grow to like you. It's the first impression that counts and it must be good. You don't have a second chance to make a first impression.

To Script or Not to Script

I observe a negative emotional reaction on the part of many salespeople to the word *canned*. And I certainly am not advocating word-for-word presentations unless they have proved to work best for you. But openers are something else. The words and the whole manner of approach should be carefully planned. You have only a few seconds to a couple of minutes to get a positive response. Why risk giving it anything but the very best performance you can create, learn, and test-prove? The words will be used over again many times. Much of your precious selling time is on the line. Any one contact may eventually be one of the biggest sales you ever make. Go with the best!

There are two types of temperament involved here. When something as important as an opener needs to be said, some people prefer to carefully select their words. Furthermore, they are disciplined enough to pay the price it takes to diligently rehearse them. Others, and probably a great majority of salespeople fall into this category, are unwilling to do so. This is especially true of those with extrovert tendencies. Carefully preparing and rehearsing what to say is contrary to their nature. It is difficult, boring, time-consuming, and ego-deflating. On the other hand, there is some self-satisfaction in believing one can ad-lib brilliantly and succinctly. True, some can. But they are indeed rare birds.

Which type are you? Weigh the price you pay (of a little time and effort, planning, and rehearsing) against these advantages:

- You will be more effective and set more appointments with the right buying authority, under the most favorable circumstances.
- It will be easier for you to give openers.
- Your attention can be concentrated on observing the prospect's reactions and less on thinking about what you're going to say. You will be able to listen better and observe nonverbal signals. These give clues as to subsequent responses you make and directions you take.
- A favorable impression up front will have long-standing favorable effect on the ensuing stages of making the sale.
- You will be more confident and poised knowing that what you're doing and saying is your best shot. This will help to dissolve any traces of fear or call reluctance.

On the other hand, here are some disadvantages to ad-libbing openers:

- They are usually longer and more rambling than necessary. Extroverted salespeople tend to be overfriendly and more talkative than good judgment would recommend in an opening situation. They are bent on selling themselves. Their reasoning is if it can be done in one hundred words, then one thousand words should be ten times better. They don't realize that a busy, possibly less extroverted prospect may not be in the mood for that much friendliness and conversation. Nor do they realize how much faster they would sell themselves if they got to the point with a benefit the prospect could quickly understand. And they don't realize how unlikely it is for prospects to have the patience to track the meaning of a long-winded monolog, how much more likely it is for them to prejudge negatively and dismiss the visitor in order to get back to their preoccupation.
- Weasel words and phrases tend to creep in. Theodore Roosevelt is credited with coining the term to describe "words that destroy the force of a statement by equivocal qualification as a weasel ruins an egg by sucking out its content while leaving it superficially intact." *Might, maybe, perhaps* fall into this category. So do phrases such as "I just happened by," "I was wondering if," "I think you ought to," and "Sorry to bother you, but. . . ."
- I-oriented phrases, instead of you-oriented phrases, tend to predominate; for example, "I'd like to show you," "I want you to see."
- Prospects will later recall a negative reaction to an opener. You destroy what you need most in a presentation—their confidence that you know what you are talking about. They may have agreed to continued dialog out of curiosity or whim, but the effect of an otherwise good presentation could be diminished.
- When you must think about what to say, you are less able to keep all senses tuned in to the moment. Vital clues can be missed.
- You are apt to experience a higher level of anxiety caused

by using needless mental energy. Remember the fable of the centipede:

> A centipede was happy quite
> Until a frog in fun
> Said, ''Pray, which leg comes after which?''
> This raised her mind to such a pitch,
> She lay distracted in the ditch
> Considering how to run.

The most legitimate reason for not scripting is that whether read from a script on the phone or memorized for in-person delivery, scripted openers tend to sound canned. You may recall the times when you get phone calls from someone trying to sell you something who is obviously reading a script. You are not impressed. Nor are most others on the receiving end of such canned pitches. What is being said nonverbally is that the person making the call doesn't know much about the product being sold. And that's probably true. There is high turnover in certain telemarketing operations because rejection rates are high. So it's likely the caller hasn't been on the job long enough to sound professional. Successful telemarketers, the ones who survive long enough to learn adequate product knowledge, are smart enough and experienced enough to grow out of the canned sound even though they may have a script in front of them.

You certainly don't want to sound like the inexperienced script reader or like an elementary school pupil reciting in class. There is nothing more critical than the sound of confidence in your voice that you have important information and that you know what you are talking about. Let's consider the elements of an effective, confident sound.

Compose in Conversational Style

There is a difference between written language and spoken language. Written language is more formal. We are careful with grammar and use bigger words than those ordinarily used in conversation.

We learned to speak before we learned to write. Speaking is a natural means of communication. Writing is synthetic. Therefore, spoken words sound natural and written words sound contrived unless special effort is taken to make them sound natural.

As you compose the scripted words, close your eyes. Compose the words in your mind as you imagine speaking them. Then open your eyes and put the words on paper. Spoken words are not necessarily as grammatically precise as written words. Grammatical precision or freedom is an individual thing. It must be something you are comfortable with. Some people speak with more precision than others.

Use words you would naturally use in spontaneous speech. Work at making it sound just as though it were coming right off the top of your head.

Choose words that your prospects easily understand and identify with as an important part of their world. I've heard insurance agents speak of capital conservation, capital needs analysis, and liquidity analysis. Although those terms refer to important benefits, some prospects might wonder where they would keep it if they ever bought it! Everyday English would be more easily understood, such as, "Let me take a look to see if you're paying too much to Uncle Sam," or "Let's try to figure out how to make sure the ownership of your property stays with your family."

Another common difference between scripted material and normal conversation is that scripted material tends to take on a singsong quality when delivered. This probably stems from recitation habits acquired in earlier school years. Listen closely to airline cabin attendants as they read the preflight safety instructions. You will hear a melody actually being sung. Talk to them later—no more melody. It doesn't happen in normal conversation.

Tip for Conversational Sound

A common and glaring error that inexperienced speakers make with scripted material is in the way the articles *a* and *the* are pronounced. In conversation, most people pronounce *a* with a short sound as the *u* is pronounced in *up*. *The* is pronounced with the same sound unless the very next syllable is a vowel. Then it is pronounced *thee*.

But when a piece is being read, the *a* often gets a long sound as in *way*. Most readers will pronounce *the* as *thee* regardless of whether or not a vowel is the immediately following sound. Since memorized material is usually learned from reading a written script, the tendency is to pronounce *a* and *the* with long sounds even though the same person would pronounce them differently in conversation. And that's a tip-off the words are being read or have been memorized from a script.

Mind Your Diction

Slurred, sloppy diction is common in our society today. I have difficulty understanding some people who run words together in such a way that it's hard to tell where one word ends and another begins. You could have a tremendously important benefit, but if the prospects can't understand you, they become uncomfortable listening to you. They want to get rid of that uncomfortable feeling. The obvious way to do that is get rid of you. Both you and the prospect lose.

What does the word AMANA mean? Is it the name of a kitchen appliance? A town in Iowa? A religious group? Yes, it is all of those. Now put the accent on the first syllable and pronounce the first a as in the a in mark. Now it is slurred diction for, "I am going to." As in, "Amana get up early tomorrow." "Amana make a sale on this next call."

When you hear *amana* used this way you probably know what it means because it is so common. But how many other *amanas* are there in your speaking style? Do you habitually run words together in ways that may be understandable to you or to your family and close friends, but not to strangers? In selling that can be costly.

Speed Zone Ahead

What about the speed of your words? What have you heard about fast-talking salespeople? They are not to be trusted, right?

Most people will feel comfortable listening to you at a speaking rate of 140 words per minute. To determine this speed, read a prepared text containing 700 words and time it. It should take five minutes to average the desired speed. If your normal rate is faster or slower, practice until you get a feel for the 140-word rate. It is important, however, to keep in step with the people you are speaking with. If they speak slower, slow your rate down. If they give indication of a hearing problem, speak a little louder. If they speak faster, speed up. Fast-talking prospects can easily become impatient with slow-talking salespeople, while slower-talking ones become suspicious of fast talkers.

Another common speech habit some people have, which suggests a lack of confidence, is to make a statement that ends on a vocal upswing making it sound like a question. The unspoken question seems to ask, "Am I OK with you so far?"

Your Eyes Tell on You

In addition to the smile we considered earlier, eye contact is another must. We think of our eyes as sensing organs and, of course, they are. But they are more than that. Your eyes can talk even though their language is silent. When they are shifting around, they are announcing a shifty character. An alarm sounds with your host saying, "Proceed with caution."

When eyes can meet another person's with sincerity and warmth, they are saying, "Here is a sincere and friendly person worth trusting."

I hope I've convinced you of the importance of a planned, yes, scripted opener—unless you are one of those rare, brilliant ad-libbers. Now comes the learning and rehearsing part.

Be a Pro

Selling is a profession. Other professions require vigorous, disciplined practice in vital skills. Could you imagine a surgeon ad-libbing through an operation—performing it differently every time to suit mood or whim? I wouldn't suggest that you climb on an operating table and put yourself in the hands of such a doctor. A skilled surgeon doesn't have to think about every movement. Likewise a professional athlete, airline pilot, musician—or a centipede.

Bill Gove, the dean of sales motivational speakers and founding president of the National Speakers Association, uses the phrase *effortless effort* to describe the physical, mental, and emotional state he wants to achieve in order to perform at his best in front of an audience. I was with Bill one day when he spent all morning rehearsing a speech he had given hundreds of times before and was to give again that day at a luncheon.

When I mentioned to Bill my surprise that he still works this hard, he replied,

Even though I have over thirty-five years on the speaking circuit, I need to practice in order to perform at my best. But this is not unusual. I've always been interested in what makes for "star quality performance" in any field, be it sports, entertainment, business, whatever. It will always include desire, tremendous energy, and persistent hard work. I practice so my audience will be more comfortable with me. But moreover, so that I will be more comfortable with me.

What a great inspiration for salespeople to learn their craft. Especially when it comes to the all-important business of performing an effective opener. Yes, it is important that we work at helping prospects to be comfortable with us during that crucial moment. But it is more important that we are comfortable with ourselves. We either pay the price of working at developing a strong, smooth opener, or pay the price of losing opportunities to sell in order to indulge in spontaneous mutterings that often fail to get the job done. That is a far greater price. You will lose a lot less time learning to do it right than you will lose making calls that are unproductive.

Audiocassette recorders are an inexpensive, convenient, and effective tool in helping you to polish your delivery. Record your opener. Listen to the playback. Does it sound like your natural conversational style? Or is it obvious that you are reading a script? Are you using bigger words than you naturally would? Is there a singsong quality that shouldn't be there? Just by identifying it, you are a long way toward eliminating it. Check the way you pronounce the articles *a* and *the*. Is that the way you always pronounce them?

Is it easily understood? Are there any slurred *amanas*? This may sound like a contradiction. On one hand it's important to use your natural conversational style. On the other hand it's important to eliminate slurred diction. If your natural style is slurred, you need to resolve the contradiction by working at changing your style.

It's difficult to be objective about our own voice. We can easily understand our own slurred diction. But can a stranger understand it? Have someone else listen to and critique your recorded version. Is it clearly understandable without sounding as though you are reading a script? If not, record it over until it is.

Then listen to it over and over until it becomes a natural part of you. If you spend a lot of time behind the wheel of your car, this is an excellent time to put your recorder to work.

Much of my time is spent in airports and on airplanes. I always carry a pocket-size recorder with a headset. It's an easy way for me to learn new speech and seminar material. It's not even necessary to listen with complete concentration. The words and the vocal inflections register on the subconscious through sheer repetition.

Video recording equipment is now quite common and inexpensive. If you have access to it, so much the better. As a training and coaching tool, I find it unbeatable. Its advantages are obvious.

Now let's talk about fine-tuning the call.

Get the Proper Setting

Ward Bergquist is a media buyer for Advance Advertising Agency. Word is out that Advance has a big budget for print from one of its clients. Ward is besieged with reps calling on him and is beginning to feel a great deal of pressure because he is getting behind schedule. Most of the reps are from publications whose demographics only marginally fit the strategy Advance's creative staff has planned for its client. To make matters worse, the reps take up a lot of time with small talk.

Ward's office walls are covered with awards the agency has won, along with framed reprints of award-winning ads. Rep after rep scrutinize them oohing and aahing, thinking that this is the way to make points. But while this is going on, Ward is only fuming. Long ago he wanted to get rid of the decorations but the president of the agency insisted on keeping them to impress clients and potential clients being solicited. To stop this intolerable waste of time, Ward told the receptionist that he would meet all reps in the lobby and conduct his business out there.

Brent Douglas represents a fairly new magazine whose demographics are perfect for the Advance client. This magazine's circulation got off to an amazing start and its editors were planning a theme for an upcoming issue that would tie in to the ad campaign. Brent has a good presentation to tell this story with a flip chart and beautifully prepared and compelling visual proof.

When he came to call on Advance, Ward quickly motioned for him to sit down in a reception lobby chair with shoulder-high sides. Ward sat in a similar chair next to him. The seats seemed to sink down almost to the floor. The chair sides were like a wall between them. The lobby was busy with phones ringing and other reps coming and going. Then a grade school class came through on a tour of "The World at Work."

Brent's presentation was a disaster! He missed an opportunity for a sale that should have been made. Ward Bergquist missed out on an excellent buy for his client.

The notion of setting up an appointment for a presentation on the right basis was mentioned previously. The preceding little vignette illustrates what can happen when you don't take the initiative to do so. You work under a serious if not impossible handicap when the setting is not appropriate.

To proceed beyond the opener at an office rail or a doorway or in any circumstances which are uncomfortable for you or the prospect is asking for a washout. It is hopeless to attempt to present visual material in a stand-up presentation or in a situation like the one in which Brent Douglas found himself. You are up to bat and the pitcher is throwing pitches that are impossible to hit. Reception lobbies with all their distractions, including other salespeople looking over your shoulder as you present, are likewise a poor setting. The only reason ever to use a lobby would be if any other alternative is less favorable—if, for example, your prospect's office or work area is a more distracting place.

It's not unusual for a prospect to invite you to sit down in a reception lobby and expect you to complete your call there. While it may be all right to state your opener out there, it is not wise to go beyond it without taking the initiative to suggest a better setting. Your proposition is too important to risk anything but the best. Believe that! When you neglect to ask for a better setting, you are nonverbally suggesting that what you have to offer is so casual that it is compatible with a casual setting.

When you suggest moving to a more appropriate place, include in your reason for doing so a benefit to the prospect. Point out that it can be given in less time or that visual and demonstration material are better seen at a desk or on top of some kind of display space. If the prospect's office is occupied or is a distraction, try for a conference room or any other place with some privacy. If the prospect's reason for denying use of the inner office is the pressure of a heavy workload or the presence of visitors with whom the prospect will be tied up for a while, you are better off to schedule an appointment for another time. Under these circumstances you're not likely to get proper attention anyway.

DOS AND DON'TS TO FINE-TUNE YOUR OPENER

DO

Relax
Be yourself
Smile
Maintain eye contact
Be confident
Be friendly but not overfamiliar
Be positive but gentle
Let your belief show
Show pride in your offering
Be sure you have the right
   buying authority
Be flexible

Maintain the initiative
Offer a benefit
Be brief
Show genuine interest in your
   prospect
Remember your objective
Ask for an appointment
Show respect for the prospect's
   time
Be prepared for resistance
Request sufficient time for your
   presentation

DON'T

Be cocky
Be apologetic
Be demanding
Be evasive
Be shifty with your eyes
Disguise the fact you have
   something to sell
Be pushy
Be hurried into an abbreviated or
   stand-up presentation
Get angry or upset

Get drawn into an argument
Sound like a sixth grader reciting
   in class
Get defensive
Be too polished
Use manipulative tricks
Plead like a beggar
Exaggerate
Try to sell your whole story in the
   opener

You Don't Need a Crutch

The sorriest reception lobby scenario is one I've seen often enough to realize it needs to be mentioned here. It goes like this: A prospect comes out to the lobby. In one of the sales rep's extended hands is a stack of note pads with the company's logo. In the other are some brochures. "I thought you might have some use for these note pads. And here is some literature about our products. If you ever need any or if you ever want some more information, give me a call. Uh, here is my card."

Incredible? It happens. If you've spent a fair amount of time in a reception lobby, you know it does. Don't you wonder what gets written on a daily report after a call like that?

Note pads with a logo are excellent for remembrance advertising. In most cases, brochures or catalog sheets or other kinds of literature are a must. However, I recommend to my clients' sales managers that they know how such sales aids are being used. Note pads, when used, are to be given out at the end of a presentation. Literature may be part of the visual material used in a presentation, but even better as a leave-behind.

Giveaways are a holdover from days gone by when door-to-door selling was more prevalent. They were called door openers and were a good idea, because residential prospects are often more wary of strangers coming to call. Door openers are not necessary in the business world. To professional buyers and executives, calls by salespeople are part of the daily routine, and door-opening gifts suggest that you really don't have much else going for you. Besides, they don't want to feel obligated. Your best door opener is an idea that offers a benefit.

Another crutch that prevails in selling is the misguided notion that the way to build rapport with someone is to select an outstanding feature on display, such as a trophy, a picture, or an indication of a hobby, and use that as a warm-up conversation starter.

While it's true that some people you call on will enjoy or at least tolerate such small talk, in the busy business and professional world, it's a serious mistake to assume that everybody does. In fact, most do not, especially with strangers, when they are pressed for time, and when they suspect that you are really not that enthusiastic about their special interest and you are only showing interest for effect. Your odds are always in favor of getting right down to the business at hand. Again, your best warm-up is a hot idea that offers a nice warm benefit. Then suggest or probe for ways your prospect can realize there is a need for the benefit and how that need can be satisfied. Even when you have someone who likes small talk, you are using up precious time with it. If the prospect is on a tight schedule the time could run out before you have a chance to complete your agenda.

The Right Kind of Enthusiasm

One of my clients, who is based in Dallas, told me this story, which takes place during a great season the Dallas Cowboys were having:

> I like to get to the office about a half-hour before office hours begin, have a cup of coffee, and read the morning paper. A rep who sells materials-handling equipment learned of my habit and came to pay me a call during my quiet time one Monday morning. This was OK with me as we were thinking about upgrading our equipment and I admire ambition in sales reps. I like to think our salespeople are doing the same.
>
> As he walked into my office he noticed I had my paper open to the sports page. The Cowboys won a game in the last few seconds the day before so he latched on to this subject supposedly to provide a warm-up to his presentation.
>
> And a good subject, too, because I'm a great Cowboys fan. His enthusiasm for the team was unrestrained. It was almost as though he were in the stands himself cheering that winning two-minute drill, and he had me right there along with him. The Cowboys are the greatest. No argument from me about that.
>
> Then we got down to business. What a letdown! When he opened his portfolio and started elaborating on his equipment, it was as if he shifted some internal gear. Oh yes, he was enthusiastic. But it was an obviously phony, contrived enthusiasm in stark contrast to the genuine enthusiasm he showed for the Cowboys. Well, we didn't buy from him, and I don't expect we will in the foreseeable future.

This rep was performing with two often misunderstood aspects of traditional sales lore. The first is, "Sell yourself first and your product second.'' This principle is valid, but be sure you sell your product with the same kind of enthusiasm as you sell yourself.

The second has to do with just what enthusiasm really is. Genuine enthusiasm must be based on genuine belief. You cannot separate the two. Enthusiasm is the verbal and physical expression of your belief in what you are selling. To act out enthusiasm is good for you to do by yourself when you are getting started in the morning or when you are feeling sluggish. It will help to perk you up. It's like an athlete's warm-up exercises. But putting on an act in front of a potential buyer in an opener situation is like telling the prospect to proceed with caution.

Be Yourself

Be yourself! This is such simple-sounding advice given to salespeople from an untold number of mentors—so simple-sounding that it seems it should be the easiest thing in the world to do. What could be more effortless than to just relax and do what comes naturally? But what a paradox when so often it doesn't turn out that way. For example, I was having breakfast with a sales rep I was to work with one day. At breakfast Bob was the most pleasant, interesting, easygoing chap. But later when faced with a prospect, Bob seemed to shift a gear and become someone else—a person who looks and sounds different from the one with whom I had breakfast. Bob became what he thinks a salesperson should look and sound like. Unfortunately, in acting out this role, Bob hides Bob, the nice guy I enjoyed chatting with at breakfast.

A common denominator in such contrived behavior is tenseness. The opposite of tenseness is relaxation. To be yourself you must be relaxed. To be relaxed is first and foremost a physical thing. Like any physical skill it can be learned.

A quick and easy relaxation technique is simply to take a deep breath, as deep as you can. Fill your lungs full of air, breathing deeply so that you can feel your diaphragm moving down. Hold the air for a few seconds. Then exhale slowly. As you exhale you will feel physical tension ebbing away. Do this two or three times and you will be even more relaxed.

The opposite of this is to hyperventilate. When we hyperventilate, we take quick short breaths. This happens when we are frightened, when we feel panicky, or when we are having an anxiety attack. As we continue to take quick short breaths, our heart starts to race. The adrenaline starts to flow. Our energy level increases and we are ready for fight or flight. This is a biological coping mechanism held over from prehistoric days when our ancestors needed this kind of energy to either fight or flee from common, daily life threatening situations such as saber-toothed tigers.

Selling situations are not life or death. We don't need that much adrenaline flowing. We don't need that much energy. Deep breathing intercepts hyperventilation, which in turn aborts the rest of the biological process.

If you are interested in learning more about relaxation techniques, I suggest you consult your local public library or bookstore, where you will find many excellent books available on the subject. I would recommend *You Must Relax* by Edmund Jacobson, *Release From Nervous Tension* by David Harold Fink, and *The Relaxation Response* by Herbert Benson and Miriam Z. Klipper. These books offer specific techniques you can easily learn that will help you to be more relaxed, not only in selling situations, but in all areas of your life.

In sales calls there is usually some degree of tension in the air, originating from both the prospect and the salesperson when they meet for the first time. It is part of your professional skill to know how to reduce any negative effect this tension may cause and to take the initiative to apply your mastery. Such skill begins with your ability to relax yourself. It would be impossible to bring it off without that ability.

Then too, be aware that regardless of the importance you may place on a call, it is just another incident in your prospect's long list of daily business contacts and routine. So relax and banish any thought that this or any other call will have a perilous or climactic influence on your sales career. Know in your heart that what you have to offer will be of benefit to your prospect. The best way to communicate that belief is in your own relaxed attitude of confident enthusiasm. Much persuasive power lies in a friendly, relaxed manner of greeting. It will do more than words to encourage a positive, open-minded response.

A relaxed attitude of confident enthusiasm will also suggest that you are no threat to ego, time, or budget and that you will accept the prospect's final decision, whatever it may be.

Chapter 14

SHARPENING YOUR TELEPHONE SKILLS

Can you imagine life without a telephone? Using the phone is such a familiar, everyday routine in our society. We've all been using it since we began to talk. What would anyone need to learn about using this simple instrument?

But the telephone has become so familiar that we take it too much for granted. We ordinarily use it without a second thought to any necessary technique. That may be all right for everyday routine calls. But to be effective in catching the attention and interest of preoccupied strangers requires planning, strategy, and discipline.

The Difference in Telephoning

Most of the basic methods of in-person openers dealt with so far apply to the telephone as well. The difference in approach has to do with three main considerations. First of all, the spoken word and along with it, the quality, speed, and tone of voice take on a new measure of importance. Second, neither you nor the prospect can see what is going on. You lose the communicative impact of body language and you lose the opportunity to gather information from any other physical signs. And third, there are particular stresses commonly associated with sustained telephone use for which you must be prepared. There is a much faster pace to telephone contact. Rejection comes quicker. Its cumulative effect takes a heavier emotional toll on most salespeople. Mobility and change of pace afforded by traveling from one call to another aren't there. Of course, this last item is a concern during sustained phone activity, not for an occasional call.

Some products and services can be presented and sales closed over the telephone. These would include items whose grade qualities are easily described such as commodities, repeat items that buyers are familiar with, and special offers such as price reduction or any extra benefit that can be offered on a temporary basis.

With products that require a personal call to close a sale, the telephone can be used to gather information, qualify prospects, and make appointments. It is important to establish your objective before each call. Decide just exactly what you want to happen.

Develop a Pleasing Voice

Regardless of the objective of a phone call, your voice is a predominant factor that will help you or hurt you. Let's zero in on it. A friendly conversational tone is fundamental. If your natural speaking style is too fast, too slow, too loud, too soft, slurred, or otherwise out of step with the person on the other end of the line, you will need to make a special effort to modify it. Your friends may be tolerant of such imperfections, but don't expect prospects to be.

Actually, 140 words per minute is somewhat slower than most people naturally speak. But the telephone tends to accentuate speed. A voice usually sounds faster to the person listening than it really is. People tend to tune out fast-talking strangers on the phone. Since the voice predominates and body language is absent, poor diction stands out all the more on the phone. It is uncomfortable to listen to someone who is difficult to understand. The natural tendency for a prospect who feels uncomfortable listening to a difficult-to-understand salesperson is to terminate the conversation as quickly as possible. Any excuse will do as long as it serves to get rid of the uncomfortable feeling, even though what is being said would be beneficial.

Check the pitch of your voice. Is it too high? If so, take any object from your desk, such as a pen or a piece of paper, and put it on your lap. Look at it as you talk and pitch your voice at it. The pitch of your voice will move downward. A lowered voice sounds warmer and more friendly.

Practice using your friendly telephone sales personality whenever you pick up the phone, not just when talking to prospects. For example, how do you talk to salespeople who call you on the phone? How about your children's friends, people below you in status, people you don't particularly like? To acquire the habit of a pleasing, friendly telephone voice, it is important to use it at all times.

Confidence—The Most Important Quality

Warmth and friendliness are desirable voice qualities, but this does not mean you should sound subservient in any way. In fact, the most important quality is the sound of confidence grounded in a deep conviction that you know what you are talking about and that you believe it will benefit the prospect. The more genuine the certainty in your voice, the more likely the prospect will want to hear you out.

Let me repeat something that was written in an earlier chapter: *It is imperative that you see yourself as a competent, knowledgeable expert in your field and that you have information and ideas that will be of benefit to the people you call on.*

The practical application of this image of yourself at the

point of contact with a prospect is the single most powerful, compelling, persuasive force when using the telephone. To fail to understand its importance is to fail to open doors to selling opportunity. Remember your positive affirmations. Repeat them as part of your precall preparation. Repeat them whenever you feel your confidence slipping.

Use a Script

Prospects are prone to make the decision of whether or not to allow a conversation to continue quicker on the phone than in a face-to-face opener. They permit interruptions in the middle of tasks for which they would not in a face-to-face call. Granted that choice of words is critical in a face-to-face call, it is even more so on the phone. An important advantage of using a phone, therefore, is that you can use a script. Make liberal use of marginal and parenthetical notes on your script regarding inflections, emphasis, pauses, and other nonverbal signals. Then practice and listen to your tape-recorded playback until you deliver it effortlessly with a natural, spoken sound. At some point, from repetitive use, you will probably have the script memorized. Nevertheless, keep it in front of you when calling. It frees your mind to make other observations and to plan how to proceed. Of course, the content of a telephone script will depend on the objective of the call.

The emphasis in this chapter is on making initial telephone contact with selected business prospects for the purpose of gathering information, qualifying the prospects, identifying needs, and making appointments for personal calls on qualified prospects.

How to Get Information

Some of the information gathering can be done before you get to the person you eventually want to reach. It is easier to get relevant information from subordinates by phone than in person. They don't know who you are. You could be a customer seeking information or someone else within their company. If the person you have on the line can't tell you what you want to know, ask for someone who can. When you don't know the name of the person you want, use dialog similar to that suggested in Chapter 11. By phone, it's easier to get through to those who can give you information and you avoid starting off on the wrong foot with your ultimate prospect. Just as it is easier for prospects to terminate a contact on the phone, the same goes for you. Use that to your advantage when it is wise to do so. Often it is better to hang up, courteously, of course, when you get the information you want and call back another time to get through to the right person. Then there will be more certainty in your approach and you're less likely to get sidetracked.

Getting to the Right Person

OK. You have enough preliminary information, including the name of the person you want. Let's say it's James Madison. You dial the number. The phone rings and someone answers with, "Good morning, Madison Company."

You don't know who answered. It could be Mr. Madison. It could be a receptionist, a secretary, or just anybody who happened to pick up the phone. Regardless, the first thing you say is:

"Mr. Madison, please."

Notice there is no question mark at the end of that statement. It's a statement, so it shouldn't sound like a question. The most common opening line salespeople use on the phone goes something like this, "Is Mr. Madison in?" That sounds like you don't know much about the comings of goings of Mr. Madison. Making it a statement will prompt fewer chances of being asked questions about the nature of your business, thus less possibility of getting sidetracked.

Now the person who answered the phone may ask you to identify yourself, which you do by merely giving your name. You may then be asked to identify your company, which you do. Take note that at this point you are giving only the information for which you are asked. After you give your name and again after you identify your company, say without pausing, "May I speak with Mr. Madison, please." You may get a third request that takes the form of, "May I tell Mr. Madison what this is about?"

Let's say your objective is to speak directly with Mr. Madison to qualify him as a prospect or get some information regarding his needs before you decide whether or not you want to make an appointment with him at this time. When asked the nature of your call by the person who answered the phone, say something like this: "The purpose of my call is to find out if our company would have any business with Mr. Madison. May I speak with Mr. Madison, please."

When your objective is to get an appointment, reply with: "The purpose of my call is to introduce myself to Mr. Madison, state my business, and arrange an appointment. May I speak with Mr. Madison, please."

Sometimes at this point you will get diverted to someone other than Mr. Madison. The secretary will say, "I'll let you speak with Mr. Monroe."

Be prepared to come back immediately, before the switch is made. Find out Mr. Monroe's title and his position in the company. Get as much information as you can about his decision-making credentials so you know where you stand.

When you are using a referral or you are asked for further clarification of the nature of your business, proceed along the same lines suggested in Chapter 12 for dialog with secretaries and assistants regarding those situations. Be sure to end each statement with, "May I speak with Mr. Madison, please."

Flexibility Requires Good Judgment

The techniques suggested here are not inflexible. There may be good reason why you would want to give more information to persons screening your call. You may be responding to an inquiry. There may be recognizable prestige to the organization you represent. You may have reason to believe that Mr. Madison would be especially interested in talking to you. Good judgment should prevail.

Reaching the Unreachable

It is helpful to have direct line numbers of prospects who are hard to reach. Most larger organizations have direct line numbers for personnel with phones at their desk or workstation. These numbers can be accessed directly from the outside without going through a switchboard or other main answering point.

Here's a common situation. Every time you call for Mr. Madison, he's not available. His secretary may be screening you out, but not necessarily. It could be that Mr. Madison is a busy person who, in fact, is often out of his office. When he is there, he's often in conferences or staff meetings.

Ask the secretary when he is most likely to be available. If she is vague about that, or if you call back at the times she suggests and still don't reach Mr. Madison, thank her and hang up gracefully.

Now dial the main answering point. Ask the receptionist/operator, "Would you please give me Mr. Madison's direct line number?" Receptionists or operators will most likely give the number to you if you ask for the number unhesitatingly, assertively. After all, it makes their job easier if callers have direct line numbers. It takes a lot of pressure off the central point. In fact, that is the main reason companies have direct lines. Some receptionists will voluntarily give you that number whether or not you ask for it. Then ask, "By the way, what time does Mr. Madison usually arrive in the morning? What time does he leave at the end of the day?" Most executives work more than an eight-hour day. Some get in before the office staff arrives. If they come in late, they usually stay late.

The reason to get this information from the main answering point is that if the secretary is screening you out, there may be a reluctance to give it to you.

You can now call your prospect early or late on the direct line. Sooner or later you will reach your intended prospect. You almost never offend prospects when you do this. If they have salespeople, they wish theirs were working the same hours. If what you sell involves your personal service, they will want to do business with someone who is on the job early or late. In other words, you will earn their respect.

Make it point to try to get a direct line number the first time you call a prospect. Just before the receptionist is going to ring Mr. Madison's number on your first call ask, "Does Mr. Madison have a direct line number?" If the answer is yes, ask, "Would you please give it to me?" Then keep the number in your prospect information file for future reference.

Should You Ask to Have Your Call Returned?

If you are unable to reach Mr. Madison at the time you place the call, you are most likely to be asked, "Is there a message you wish to leave for him?" You want to talk with him directly, so there isn't any intermediate message. What you are really being asked is, "Do you want Mr. Madison to return your call?"

Some people diligently return every phone call; others return a call only when they can identify the caller or have reason to believe the call is one they want to take.

If you are a typical salesperson, you don't spend much time sitting in the office with an open phone waiting for someone to call. You are either out making in-person calls or using your phone. So generally speaking, it's better not to have calls returned by prospects, at least not until you've made several attempts at direct contact. But when the only way to get through to your right person is to have the call returned, then make arrangements for that.

Your Prospect Is on the Line

Now you have Mr. Madison on the line. Your opener to him will contain the same three parts as with an in-person opener, that is: (1) an introduction of yourself and your company, (2) an opening benefit, and (3) a request for an appointment. But now we add a couple of optional requests, for a telephone interview or presentation if you intend to close the sale on the phone.

Introductions take on special importance on the phone because he can't see you. Two questions are in his mind right from the start: Who is calling? And is it someone I'm supposed to know? You need to answer those questions quickly and clearly before you say anything else. Otherwise he may not listen to what you say. He will be distracted by searching for answers to those questions in his mind. This doesn't happen in person because then these questions are answered by sight.

If Mr. Madison answers with "Hello" or anything other than his name, you begin with, "Mr. Madison, please." Remember that is a statement, not a question. If he answers the first time with his name or responds to your first statement with yes or, "This is he," repeat his name but this time add his first name or initials and now make it sound like a question. When he responds again with yes, reply with, "Thank you." Repeat his name again, introduce yourself, and continue with the opener. The sequence would go like this:

Mr. M.: Hello.

You: Mr. Madison, please.

Mr. M.: This is he.

You: Mr. James Madison?

Mr. M.: Yes.

You: Thank you, Mr. Madison. My name is Pat Murphy with Acme Corporation. Mr. Madison, my company is serving many manufacturing firms with an idea that our customers find substantially reduces hours of labor on certain manufacturing processes. My special purpose in calling you today is to find out if it would have an application to your business. Would this be a good time to get your answers to a few questions?

Remember to insert a benefit statement before asking if this is a good time to talk. Remember, too, that people will often allow the telephone to interrupt tasks for which they would not allow interruptions on an in-person call. Therefore it is important to check their availability early on. Sometimes they will pick up the phone because they were expecting some other important call. When they find out it's you instead, that would not be a good time for you to continue. You want to find that out and when you do, back off. Offer to call another time. Ask for a suggestion as to when it would be better to call.

Variations of the Script

The techniques covered earlier for situations when you don't know the name of the right person—using referrals, offering benefit statements, qualifying, probing for needs, avoiding prejudgment, and closing for appointments—apply on the telephone as well. Compose variations to suit your objective, whether it is to qualify a prospect, identify needs, arrange an appointment, or close a sale. Be sure to keep in the forefront of your mind the importance of an effective benefit statement. It is the key to your right to be heard. The first drafts of your script are not likely to be the final product. As you use a script you will discover better words to use, better approaches.

Editing the Script

When editing look for ways to simplify and keep it short. If you can establish a firm foundation of interest in thirty seconds with a strong benefit, you have a great advantage. Busy people will often honor a request for a half-minute on the phone. If the conversation goes beyond that, it's because they want to hear more. Tell them so up front.

Refine your script to cut out unnecessary words and

phrases. Cut out weasel words. Replace longer, hard-to-pronounce words with those that are shorter, easier to pronounce. Longer words are more likely to be misunderstood. If your prospect doesn't follow the meaning easily, interest is lost, and along with it a sales opportunity. Make sure your benefit stands out in bold relief.

Do your editing by listening to the tape-recorded version. Ask yourself, does it sound like written or spoken language? Is the meaning clear? Avoid any stretch more than fifteen seconds long. Break up longer stretches with questions. Have a separate script sheet with a variety of typical questions and be prepared to use them for any contingency. After asking a question, shut up and listen.

Open-end questions are especially important on the phone. In face-to-face situations you have material, body language, and perhaps demonstrations to help sustain interest. None of this is there to work for you on the phone. Therefore, you need to make extra effort to get more active participation from prospects. Open-end questions will help you to do this. Review all of the questioning techniques learned in Chapter 8.

Setting Appointments

When your objective is to get an appointment, take the lead in suggesting times to get together. Don't hesitate on this point. Hesitation can mean missed opportunity. During an in-person opener you have the option of continuing with a spot interview or presentation. A parallel situation on the phone is to offer to come over right away if that is convenient for both parties. This is especially wise when the prospect has shown some initial resistance.

As you know, not all appointments hold up. Boyan's law states, "The firmness of an appointment diminishes with the square of the time elapsed between the opener and the appointment date." The old saw "Strike while the iron is hot" fits here. The benefits you emphasized that lessened the prospect's reluctance tend to be quickly forgotten. The more time that has elapsed, the greater the chance that something will turn up in a prospect's world to compete with that time slot. The sooner you follow up with an appointment, the better.

When an appointment is set for another week it may be a good idea to reconfirm it. I say, may be, to suggest caution. On the one hand, Boyan's law takes effect and makes it seem wise to reconfirm. But on the other hand, another telephone contact with a prospect gives him or her an opportunity to beg off.

To lessen the chance of appointments becoming unglued, take some extra precautionary measures at the outset. When you get a verbal agreement on time and date say something like this: "Mr. Madison, I'm now writing down on my calendar 8:00 A.M. on May 6. Would you please do the same so we can both be sure to have it right? I have 8:00 A.M. on May 6, OK?"

When you call back to reconfirm, do it the day before the appointment is scheduled. It's best to have someone call for you or try to confirm it with a secretary. If you get Mr. Madison on the line instead, quickly come to the point, confirming time and place, and end the call politely but without unnecessary conversation. If he tries to beg off, be prepared to resell, coming out with benefits again. If that doesn't keep the original date firm, come right back with suggested alternative dates.

Another good way to help keep an appointment firm is to drop a note in the mail (a postcard will do) as a reminder. Lead off your message with a thank-you and restate the benefit something like this: "Thank you, Mr. Madison, for agreeing to get together with me on May 6. I promise to leave you with several good ideas which our clients have found reduce their manufacturing costs. See you at 8:00 A.M. sharp."

Precall Letters

An effective technique that helps get the attention of hard-to-reach prospects is an introductory letter sent in advance of your first phone call. This letter should be short, three paragraphs on one page. It should be a personal letter that is individually typed or produced on a word processor. Avoid anything that makes it look like a mass mailing. Use a number 10 envelope, no label, and a regular postage stamp rather than metered postage. Most people open envelopes and read letters that look like this. Do not include a brochure or descriptive literature unless the product described is so revolutionary that, by itself, it would arouse curiosity. A brochure makes it look like a mass mailing. That's just what you don't want it to look like. Brochures are used in mass mailings to generate inquiries. Mass mailings can be cost-effective with certain products and services because you can send a large volume and make it profitable even with a relatively small percentage of return.

But we are not talking about mass mailings. You want to reach key prospects and make appointments with them. If mass mailings with brochures could do the job, you wouldn't need to make cold calls.

An enclosure that can be effective is an article from a magazine that tells about a problem common to prospects you call on for which you have a solution.

A phone call to a secretary, in advance of your mailing, to find out whether or not the right person will be in when your letter and follow-up call come in will greatly increase your chances. Be sure you have the correct spelling of the person's name, also that of the company. Don't abbreviate unless that is the style they use. Some people take offense at little things like that.

Confine your mailings to high-priority or otherwise hard-to-reach prospects. Don't get hooked on precall letters. Some salespeople won't pick up the phone unless a letter went out first. They find things to do other than selling when they run out of premailed prospects to follow up. On the other hand, don't send out more mailings than you can follow up in a week. The effect of such letters wears off quickly.

Here is an example of a precall letter:

Dear _____ :

Because of the undoubtedly heavy demands upon your time, I am taking this means to introduce my company and myself.

The enclosed article from *Business News Monthly* entitled "Are Your Employees Costing You Money . . . Or Making You Money?" dramatically points out how easily payroll dollars can be unnecessarily wasted. We are currently serving thousands of business firms with a simple and inexpensive supplement to management's efforts that our clients tell us has upgraded the performance of their people and reduced payroll costs substantially.

I will contact you within the next few days for an appointment at your convenience so that you may evaluate our idea in terms of profit to your organization.

When you follow up with your telephone opener, state the opener as you would had you not sent the letter. Lead with your benefit. Reminding a prospect that you sent a letter is not a good opening line. It is not a very compelling benefit. Don't use the letter as a crutch for something to say. A benefit is the most important thing you can say. Why start the game with your second string? It's better if the prospect mentions the letter first. If not, you can make reference to it and any supporting enclosure at a later point in the dialog.

To increase your chances of having a prospect take notice of your letter, send it on a fax machine, if your prospect has one, or by courier service, or U.S. Postal Service Express Mail. If you don't have a fax machine, they are available for public use at many hotels and print shops. It is more expensive to use these methods, but for high-priority prospects and in certain other instances, it may be worth the investment.

A directory of companies that accept all fax documents sent to them is published by Dial-A-Fax, Deerfield Beach, Florida (305-421-2101).

State-of-the-Art Answering Machines

Answering machines are getting more sophisticated and more widely used. Voice mail is in. When you dial the main switchboard of some companies, instead of a live operator, you get a recorded voice suggesting several options.

Some years ago, the back wall of every hotel registration area was a latticework of boxes that stored messages for each guest room. If you could imagine that through each box is a phone line connected to a computer, you are getting a picture of how voice mail works. The voice is not recorded on tape. When you leave a message, your voice is electronically changed into binary code and stored on a computer hard disk. When a prospect retrieves your message, the computer translates the code back into an exact duplicate of your voice.

One advantage for you is that you can access this equipment twenty-four hours a day, seven days a week. You can work more flexible hours, extend your working time, and for long-distance prospects, reduce your phone bills by calling during reduced-rate time. Another advantage is that when voice mail systems are used, direct line numbers are usually more freely given.

The bad news is that the systems become the ultimate screener. In too many cases, every time you punch the direct line for some prospects, you get the stored message telling you that Ms. Raimondi is not available but please leave a message.

The first thing to do is to call the central number. Use the option that gets you to a live operator. Ask if Ms. Raimondi ever answers her own phone. If so, when and under what conditions? If her policy is to not answer it, you are faced with the reality that you're not going to talk with her by phone unless she wants to talk to you and she takes the initiative to do so.

Next find out if her secretary is available by phone. She usually is. Do whatever you can to establish rapport and make her your ally. She is the intermediary needed to get Ms. Raimondi to want to call you. Bear in mind she has a responsibility to exercise some care in seeing to it that ideas and information which would benefit the company are not being screened out. Keep your dialog with her focused on what your product or service will do for the company rather than

on what it is. The issue here isn't whether or not Ms. Raimondi is going to buy what you sell, but rather whether she
will return your call so you can speak with her directly.
Convince her secretary that you are not a time waster. You
have valuable ideas, information, and experience that would
be vital to Ms. Raimondi's concerns even if she doesn't
eventually buy.

If you're not able to get to the secretary either, try to find
someone in the organization with some influence who may be
concerned with the benefits you have to offer and who can
act as an intermediary. Otherwise you are stuck with the
machine.

If the machine is the only one that will converse with you,
state your opener to it. Choose your words carefully. Rehearse and edit with a tape recorder so you will deliver it
convincingly. Now you can be creative. Play your carefully
rehearsed and final edited recorded version over the phone so
it comes across unflawed. No need to disguise the fact that it
is recorded. After all, her message is. She will give you credit
for being creative. It's sure to arouse her curiosity to the
point where she will want to listen to it all. So now you can
make it longer, get more points across than you could in a
live opener. Hopefully she will be curious enough to want to
give you a call and talk to this creative genius firsthand.

You could have someone with an authoritative voice, such
as a professional radio announcer, introduce you on the tape
and say complimentary things about you that would sound
pretentious coming from you. Have some of your best customers record testimonial messages on what you did for them
on your tape. You then have a powerful, convincing form of
the "our customers tell us . . ." line used in your opener.
This is especially effective if your endorsements comes from
someone with whom Ms. Raimondi can identify and whom
she respects. Be sure to stress what your product or service
can do for Ms. Raimondi. Most important of all, come across
as someone who is loaded with valuable information and
professional expertise. Use this recorded technique even if

you got to the secretary but still didn't get a return call from Ms. Raimondi.

You can combine this approach with the precall letter mentioned earlier. If Ms. Raimondi is a high-priority prospect who deserves more effort, send a series of mailings a few days apart. Include bits of information in each that you feel would be of interest to her. There could be exceptions, but this information ordinarily should not be about the product or service you sell, although it could be related to the use of it. The point you are trying to make is that you are a source of valuable information, you have her interest at heart, and you could be even more valuable to her if she would return your call.

Preparing for Extended Telephone Use

When using the phone regularly for long periods of time, give some attention to the physical setup of your surroundings. You can be at your best only when you're free of distraction and give the task a full measure of concentration, physically, mentally, and emotionally. Privacy and quiet are ideal, but this is not the case in every office. Do what you can to arrange for it.

Before you start calling, make sure everything you need is handy—writing materials, prospect files, scripts, appointment books, and anything else that makes the job go more smoothly. If you are right-handed, put the telephone to your left on the desk. Then your right hand will be free to take notes and the cord will be out of your way. For extended telephone use, some people prefer using a headset, sometimes called a star set. Then both hands are free to gesture, which helps you to speak more expressively, and to retrieve data from files. Star sets are available from the phone company or from electronics stores that sell phone equipment. If you don't have a push-button phone, get one.

In precall planning, express your objectives in terms of some end result, such as number of appointments made, number or total dollar volume of sales, number of prospects qualified. It is better to aim for these end results rather than expressing your objective as the amount of time spent on the phone.

Get your prospect cards stacked in advance. During the planning stage is the time to make decisions as to whom you're going to call and in what order. Once you start calling, keep dialing one call after another until you've reached your goal or it's time to take a break. Schedule ten minutes of break time each hour; it's important to stay fresh.

Not every call will be productive, but some percentage will. Keep in mind, though, that every call contributes to the final goal. The law of averages is working. Even when several in a row are disappointing, you will have to get through those to uncover the productive ones. To that extent, those calls were successful. So keep dialing.

Keep a record of the number of calls you need to make to produce a certain number of appointments, which results in so many dollars of sales or commission. Let's say it takes ten calls, including prospects who are unavailable, to get one appointment. You sell one out of three appointments for an average commission of $200. Then each call earns you about $6.60 whether you reach a prospect or not. Think about that as you dial.

The bane of telephone success is the ease with which you can find things to do other than dialing the next number—such things as rearranging prospect cards, talking with an associate, or stopping to figure out what is wrong. Usually nothing is wrong. It's just that the law of averages is giving you one kind of streak. It happens. The cumulative effect of repeated "not in," "too busy," "not interested" builds up much faster on the phone than in person. Be prepared to accept this as a fact of life. It would be nice if they were spread out evenly, but they are more likely to come in bunches. Your best bet to even things out is to keep dialing.

On the other hand, setting an appointment or closing a sale enhances your ability to be physically, mentally, and emotionally effective. Now you've gained momentum. By continuing activity, this motivating power of momentum will go to work for you. This is not the time to let up. If you do, the force of constant activity upon which momentum depends is gone.

Record Information

When you have a prospect on the line, be sure to write down all the pertinent information you hear—things like when purchases are likely to be planned in the future, what needs were disclosed, names of buying influentials. Write down comments for which you may want clarification or feedback from the prospect later. When an appointment is made, confirm the address and get directions if you're not sure of the location.

If you need to have a variety of scripts depending on what the prospects' needs are and you don't know which one to have ready, here is an idea. Have each script on a separate sheet of paper and cut the sheets to varying lengths. Arrange them by length with the shortest piece on top. Put the title or identification of each sheet at the very bottom. As you look at this file only the top sheet and the titles of each page will show. It will then be easy to find the script you need.

Emotional and Physical Preparation

As you can see from this chapter, to be effective making approaches on the telephone requires a lot more than the casual attention we ordinarily give to using this commonplace instrument. In addition to learning the techniques, it takes energy and a positive mind-set. Good technique is the result of intelligent planning and the will to form sound habits. Execution is something else.

Fatigue, lack of sleep, hangovers, and a negative mental state can eradicate good technique. These are all factors which have a pronounced, conspicuous effect on the way your words sound to a prospect. And they are factors over which you have complete control. You choose to do or not to do what is necessary to be prepared physically and mentally.

Your physical and mental state will determine how you feel emotionally. To choose behaviors that assure you are well rested and not hung over is obvious. And there is no deep, dark secret to maintaining a positive attitude. Suggestions for doing that are sprinkled throughout the pages of this book. Although these suggestions apply to all phases of selling, they need to be applied most urgently when using the phone.

It is as if we had a stereo tape recording in our head. One track has positive thoughts reminding us of all the wonderful benefits of what we sell and how our prospects will be happy we came along. The other track is reminding us that people on the other end of the line are busy and resent being interrupted by pestering salespeople.

If we do not exercise conscious control of our thoughts, they will be influenced by exterior forces. When these forces are positive, they serve as a catalyst to propel us with positive energy. The volume is turned up on the positive stereo track.

But when these forces are negative, as they often are in selling, and they come faster and with greater intensity on the phone, up goes the negative volume, down goes the positive volume. Down goes our performance.

And when that happens, we must step in and take over the volume controls. In fact, the most successful salespeople form a habit of keeping their hands on the controls at all times.

Chapter 15

MORE ON RESISTANCE

How do you handle the prospect who says, "I'm not spending any money"? How do you overcome the skeptic? These are questions I often get from people in my seminar audiences. We are so answer-oriented in our society. In school, there was an answer in the back of the book. There was one right answer to every question. The smart kids and the teacher knew it. It was important to find it out before the test.

But life is not like that. There is usually a lot more to the typical real-life questions than an answer in the back of the book. This is especially true when it comes to dealing with resistance in selling.

To begin with, I take issue with the questions. Consider phrases such as "handle the prospect" and "overcome the skeptic." The words *handle* and *overcome* have a hostile sound. Put yourself in the prospect's place. How do you feel when a salesperson trying to sell you something handles or overcomes you?

Set the Right Emotional Climate

Of course we must respond to objections with words. And the choice of words is important. By all means select them with considerable deliberation. Write them down. Learn to use them. Memorize them. But those carefully selected words will not work the way you expect if the climate you set is not right, if your attitude is one of an opponent who is trying to handle, overcome, control.

Prospects make decisions to set appointments with salespeople when their emotional reaction to an opener is favorable. They use the logic found in the words to justify their decision after it is made. You get a favorable emotional reaction when prospects perceive you as a knowledgeable professional in some area of their interest who is not a threat to budget, time, or ego. That perception is largely influenced by nonverbal messages.

I've gone to great lengths in covering the knowledgeable professional aspect in this book. Let's now consider the threat aspect of the opening climate.

What About the Prospect's Fears?

Much has been said about a salesperson's fear during an opening situation, but think about the prospect. The fear of being sold acts as negatively on prospects as the fear of rejection acts on salespeople. Their ego will not allow them to admit to you that they fear that the boss, or friends, or peers will criticize or ridicule them for making a mistake. Nor would they want to admit to a fear of loss, fear of failure, fear of change. So what do they do? They make a negative remark that is a defensive tactic. They will say, "I'm satisfied with my present situation," or "I'm not interested," or "I'm too busy"—anything to get rid of the feeling of fear, which is very uncomfortable. Logic has nothing to do with this. What you are hearing in the so-called objections are smokescreens. Their purpose is to cloud up the emotional state.

You can answer those smokescreens backward and forward with the most carefully prepared pat answer in the world and you still won't get in the door on the right basis. Because what you are hearing is not the real issue. Your logic does not address the real issue, which is fear.

So what you must do is dissolve the fear or, better yet, take measures to prevent it from cropping up in the first place. You do that by just being yourself. You do it with honesty, patience, understanding, tact, friendliness, a sincere desire to be of service, and without seeing prospects as enemies or as having your commission dollars in their checking accounts.

What Goes on Inside of You?

Now back to your own emotional response. If your natural reaction is to flinch when a prospect utters a negative-sounding remark, you're reacting automatically, like Pavlov's dogs who expected food every time a bell rang. We still have a lot of prehistoric-era programming in our bodies. We don't need all that much adrenaline pumping. We don't need that much energy. When we allow that to happen, we get defensive (fight); we try to prove we're right with argument. Or we cop out (flight). Either way, nobody wins.

Arguments are primarily logical. You can win them and still lose a chance to make a sale.

The cop-out is often totally nonverbal. It isn't that a salesperson physically runs away. It's just that the conviction is gone from the way the words are delivered.

A Case of Cop-out

Ziggy Loozer is in a slump. He's way behind in his draw and just this morning for the first six calls he heard "not spending a cent," "my budget is overspent," "can't afford it," "we're cutting back," "no way," and "call back in six months." The positive stereo track in his head is disconnected. The negative one is using bad grammar—triple negatives, "nobody ain't buying nothing!" And it's blasting loud and clear.

Ziggy's next call is on Joe Crying, Manager of Crying Towel and Linen Supply Company. Ziggy figured it would help if he could do a better job of establishing rapport with his prospects first. He remembered the sales seminar last week when he learned it was a good idea to ask questions. So he thought he'd try a different opening line.

"Good morning, Mr. Crying. How's business?"

"Terrible," Crying replied, "worst it's ever been. Besides, collections are slow. We've laid off one-third of our employees and cut back all spending. Now what is it you want to see me about?"

Ziggy has some good answers to this one because he sells advertising. "Now is the time you really need advertising. It pays! It will boost the morale of your sales force. It will get you more business. It's an investment that will return a profit."

But Ziggy's negative stereo track is still playing. "Yeah, but Crying ain't got no money to spend." And when Ziggy gives out with his carefully prepared phrases, Crying doesn't believe that Ziggy has a solution to his problem for the simple reason that he can tell from the tone of his voice that Ziggy doesn't believe it either. Ziggy copped out!

An attitude of hopelessness sometimes prevails during times of economic slowdown. This negative attitude precludes the will to explore the possibility of business from sources other than the most obvious ones. It stifles creative thinking about where future business may come from and what could be done now to get an edge when that business is placed. Actually, economic recessions are times to get the jump on the competition. These are the times when competitors are likely to have their heads in the sand, when they quit doing the things that got them business during the boom years—like thoroughly covering their territories with a positive attitude.

Interpret With Care

Often a prospect's response to an opener is taken to be an objection by a salesperson when it is not. Take statements such as, "I am very busy," or "I am satisfied with my present source of supply." What do they mean? Are they objections?

A prospect may say, "I am very busy," but he may be thinking, "This sounds like something we could use. I better try to fit it into my schedule." Or "I am satisfied with my present source of supply. But maybe there is something better. I'm willing to take a look."

Because the prospect's response to your opener may be a smokescreen, or it may not really be an indication of indifference, or skepticism, or an objection, don't feel compelled to jump in and start answering it. Acknowledge the fact that you heard what was said. But do this with a noncommittal remark such as:

I understand.
I'm not sure I understand.
Oh!
Really.
Hmm.
Is that so?
I see.
That's possible.
That's OK.
That's fine.

These are all neutral comments. "I understand," is neither agreement nor disagreement. "That's OK" and "That's fine" mean that it's OK or fine with you that the prospect said what was said. It's important you stay neutral with your body language also. In other words, don't raise your eyebrows or otherwise suggest you doubt, disagree, challenge, or imply any kind of judgment on what the prospect said.

After the neutral comment, ask for clarification if you're not sure what the prospect meant, or continue probing for a need, or, if a need is revealed, expand or restate your benefit and suggest a time for an appointment.

Suppose a prospect said, "I don't believe I'd be interested."

Don't be too quick to take that at face value. And don't be

too quick with a blunt question such as, "But you would be interested in making a profit, wouldn't you?"

Ask Why Tactfully

Asking why in its various forms, as suggested in Chapter 8, is important to understand any hidden meaning lurking behind the words you hear.

But asking "Why do you say that?" can be too blunt. You want an open-end question to get the prospect to open up and tell more about where his or her interests lie. Try this form of *why:* "Obviously you have a good reason for saying that. Do you mind telling me what it is?"

If you suspect the answer to that question may be a smoke-screen, follow up with, "In addition to that, are there any other reasons why you feel you wouldn't be interested?" If the prospect says there are no other reasons, then you have only one reason to deal with. This avoids the ping-pong game in which objections keep coming up and you keep countering with answers. In fact, there is implied agreement that if that one reason were satisfied, you have a green light to proceed.

Welcome Busy Prospects

Obviously, it would not be good judgment to go through this kind of questioning when you have good reason to believe the prospect is busy at an urgent task. Bear in mind, however, that busyness is one of the most common smokescreens heard during an opener. People don't sit around just waiting for you to come selling. They're always busy doing something. You come along and interrupt the activity. They want to get back to it. So they say the first thing that comes to mind and that's "I'm busy."

Usually something in the way it is said is a tip-off as to how busy they really are. Listen for that! But don't be too quick to withdraw. If you have a person who is in the habit of saying "I'm busy" to most salespeople, you may have an excellent prospect. The competition for that person's time and budget is not as heavy as with other prospects, since few salespeople hang in there. As a matter of fact, when prospects tell you they don't have time to talk to you, and it is true, they are expressing a need to reduce their workload. If one of the benefits of your products is convenience or time saving, you may not need to do any further probing. If that benefit doesn't ring a bell, you probably have a smokescreen. When the busyness is real, suggest another time.

A good way to test for the validity of the "busyness" rejoinder is to ask, "As long as I'm here (or have you on the phone), do you mind if I get your answer to a few questions?" When prospects are truly busy, they will let you know by declining your request. If the answer is "Go ahead," proceed with your prepared qualifying questions. If answers to your qualifiers are positive, probe for when you can get together to pursue it further. Almost everyone can find some time of the day, or day of the week, that is not as busy as other times.

How to Deal With Procrastination

Another common resistance at an opener is procrastination, the tendency to put off making an appointment until some indefinite time in the future. It is important here to know what is going on. In the first place, procrastination is an almost universal human trait. Lamentably few live by the dictum "Do it now!" Most will give any excuse as long as it serves to delay a decision.

Secondly, procrastination indicates your opener is only partly effective. You stated a benefit that sounds like something that could satisfy a genuine need. Prospects don't want to close the door on it. They honestly feel they will hear you out at some future date. Yet somehow it just doesn't seem to be an urgent thing to do now.

Come back again at a later date and you can be virtually certain that whatever interest was stirred up the first time will be gone. You're not even back to square one. You're in a minus position. There's a chance your second contact is made at a less convenient time. Keep coming back often enough, you become a pest.

It is so easy for most people to procrastinate when they are faced with the decision of whether to talk to this salesperson further now or not. They will put you off if you give them the slightest encouragement to do so unless they urgently need what you are selling.

If you repeatedly get procrastination, work on making your opener stronger. Add more urgency. Urgency can be impending change in price. It can be based on availability, or lack of it—not necessarily of what you sell, but your availability. You are available now. Next week, next month you may be working another part of your territory, or involved in some other project. One of your best urgencies is the longer they delay considering your offer, the longer they delay enjoying the benefits. If you have something that increases profit, they will delay gaining profits. If you can save them money, the longer they will be spending money unnecessarily. If you have something that makes their job easier, the longer they will continue working harder than necessary.

When it's obvious to you that someone is missing out on a valuable benefit by procrastinating, here is a good spot for a "just supposing" question. For example: Just suppose you knew a prospect was using some obsolete method or equipment that was costing time and dollars. You could ask, "Just suppose I have a way to cut your payroll costs by at least 5 percent starting next week. Would you still rather wait until the next time I'm in this part of my territory?"

Emphasizing urgency based on your benefits underscores your belief in what you sell. So don't be too quick to settle for a rain check. You are there. Use good judgment in making the most of it.

Keep thinking in terms of *when* they will hear your presentation, instead of *whether*. Keep suggesting specific dates. Do it right now. Offer to come right over if you're on the phone.

You won't get through to all the procrastinators, but when you know they need what you sell, you are doing them a disservice when you are too quick to retreat. Be thankful there is such a trait as procrastination. If everything were sold because buyers always took the initiative to phone their orders or send them in the mail, there would be no need for salespeople, only order takers. Come to think of it, there would be no need for this book. I'm certainly thankful for procrastinators. They make me feel useful.

Then There Is the Skeptic

Skepticism is another resistance that is sure to be present to some degree in virtually every initial sales contact. It would be a rare person who is completely trusting of strangers, especially those who sell.

Yes, especially those who sell! It goes back to ancient Rome when the code was *caveat emptor,* which means, "let the buyer beware." That code persists today in the minds of many buyers. A popular misconception today is that all salespeople exaggerate, and their ability to do it convincingly is a measure of their sales skill. That misconception is nourished by artless salespeople who lavish their statements with meaningless generalities such as "we're the best," "the greatest," "the Number One," "you can't beat this deal." Of course, such banalities are not convincing, but that's part of the misconception.

Because exaggeration is so prevalent, all salespeople must live with the burden that some of their legitimate claims will fall upon skeptical ears. Therefore, the first step to minimizing skepticism is one of prevention. It is important to be aware of the need to build a foundation of believability, nonverbally and verbally, from the very first moment of contact. That is why such things as relaxed manner and eye contact are so vital for in-person calls, likewise voice quality and speed on the phone. You must first deal with skepticism at the emotional level before logic will have any bearing.

I would never, never advocate deception in a selling situation. You may get by with it occasionally, but sooner or later it will backfire. It usually does so at a most inopportune moment.

Abner Foonman sells leasing. His market niche is heavy equipment dealers. His approach is to call a dealer on the phone and pose as someone in the market for a bulldozer. He asks a lot of questions that give him information he needs to qualify the dealer as a prospect. He thanks the dealer and ends the conversation by saying he wants to shop around. A few weeks later he calls on the dealer with a proposal based on the information he gained under false pretenses. Abner is going to get caught with his deception, if only by suspicion. And it's likely to happen with a prime prospect who would have been one of his best customers. Now Abner is going to miss out on a lot of high-quality, profitable business over the years.

A common exaggeration that is prevalent in our verbal culture can get us into trouble in the opening sequence. We say, "It will only take a minute." Now often we don't mean exactly sixty seconds. We mean a short length of time without being specific. So the prospect agrees. Twenty minutes later we are still talking. The prospect remembered we said it would take only a minute. If we exaggerate about that, the conclusion is we probably exaggerate about a lot of other things.

It's a good idea to be specific about the amount of time you expect to take. Let's say your presentation usually takes twenty minutes. Say, "You can evaluate this idea in about twenty minutes. If I stay longer, it's because you want me to—because you have some questions beyond my presentation."

In your dialog with a skeptic make sure that what you say is believable and can be backed by proof. But don't come on too quickly and too strongly with your proof. Making prospects feel sheepish because they were wrong to show skepticism won't help your cause. Then you're in the wrong emotional zone. Logic won't mean a thing! A time-tested technique for neutralizing skepticism is the familiar "feel, felt, found" formula. It goes like this:

Mr. Jefferson, I know how you *feel.* Many of our customers have *felt* the same as you do now, when we first approached them with this idea. But they *found,* after using our system, their costs went down considerably, sometimes as much as 30 percent. For example, here is a letter we got from one of our customers, Mr. William Harrison. . . .

This is the classic model of the feel, felt, found formula. I give it here because the words *feel, felt, found* make it easy to remember. Since many salespeople have been trained to use it, I suggest changing the words when calling on experienced professional buyers, to give it a different sound. For example:

It doesn't come as a surprise to hear you say that, Mr. Jefferson. Many of our best customers said the same thing when we first approached them with this idea. Now they've been using our system for years and have realized a substantial cost reduction, in some cases as much as 30 percent. For example, here is a letter we got from one of our customers, Mr. William Harrison. . . .

Then come back with relating the benefit specifically to his situation and close for an appointment.

Other Forms of Resistance

Does Never Always Mean Never?

After your opener, prospects or secretaries may say, "We never . . .

do business with out-of-town companies."
buy anything from telephone solicitation."
buy from distributors."
hire personnel from employment agencies."
consider a source of supply such as yours, whatever the disqualifier."

Whenever you hear those kind of statements, *always* ask, "Do you ever make exceptions to that rule?" Regardless of how they answer, follow with a "just supposing" question. "Just supposing we could (specifically mention something you may be able to do better than the present sources), you would sure want to know more about it, wouldn't you?"

The Disgruntled Former Customer

You state your opener. When the prospect responds you find out it's a former customer who is unhappy with something that happened dealing with your company in the past. Here is a recommended procedure:

1. Say you are sorry to hear there was an unsatisfactory experience.
2. Ask what exactly happened.
3. Listen without interrupting, without judgment, without being defensive. Your attitude here must be one of sincere desire to understand exactly what happened. You want to find out the facts and the feelings involved. You also want some catharsis to take place. The very fact that your former customer is venting these feelings to you will go a long way to helping you build a new, positive relationship. Say, "I can understand how you feel. I don't blame you for feeling that way." Ask questions to draw out more detail.
4. Ask what he or she would like you to do to make it up.
5. Offer to go the extra mile. You would be willing to take extra care, give extra service to reestablish the business relationship. Spell out these extras in specific terms insofar as possible.
6. Put emphasis on what you can do for the prospect instead of the fact that you want the business.
7. It's helpful to get your boss involved. The higher the level of the executive in your company, the better.
8. Remember that irrationality needs to be dealt with at an emotional level. Your attitude of sincerity, honesty,

understanding, openness, willingness, vulnerability, and being nonjudgmental are the keys to reopening the door.

The Secretary Says the Boss Wouldn't Be Interested

A secretary decides the boss wouldn't be interested. She makes this decision based on only the slightest notion of what your proposition is all about. She may be right under any circumstance. Maybe the company is sold, or going out of business, or the boss is leaving the company soon, or any one of many reasons that would preclude interest in talking to you. But you don't know that. So first off, ask one of the forms of *why* suggested earlier. For example, "Obviously you have a good reason for saying that. Would you mind sharing it with me?"

If you have reason to believe her remark is a common, knee-jerk type of prejudgment, ask a just supposing question. "Just supposing I had an idea that would substantially increase your company's sales (or whatever is your best benefit), wouldn't your boss want to know about it?"

The Broken Record

You hear the same objection repeated often in response to your opener. You then need to build a rebuttal into it. Suppose prospects repeatedly say, "We prefer to do business with a local firm." In your opener include something like, "We have customers all over the country who appreciate our overnight delivery and our service reps on duty with a twenty-four-hour, seven-day, toll-free number for any special needs. Above all, they find our high-volume purchasing power saves them a substantial amount compared with their previous source of supply."

Just Send a Brochure

When a prospect or a secretary asks you to send a brochure instead of arranging an appointment, two things may be happening. Such prospects may be in the market for what you have to sell, but the time of your call may be inopportune to grant you further dialog. Most often, however, you are merely getting a brush-off. You need to know which situation you are facing. So ask:

> Whenever people ask me to send literature instead of making an appointment, I find that one of two things is happening. Either they are sincerely interested in what I have to offer and they want to know more about it, or they are not interested, and asking for literature is just another way of saying so. Just so I don't waste your time or my time, would you mind telling me the situation here?

How you say this is critical. Don't try to sound cute, clever, or tricky. And certainly don't make it sound like a demand. Selling is a vital and legitimate profession in free enterprise society. You are asking a legitimate question. You have every right to an honest answer. Remember what we said earlier— your time is just as valuable as their time! Ask the question as one business person to another—one human being to another who has every right to know.

If they are interested and want to know more about what you sell, continue with, "I will certainly do whatever you want me to do. But our brochure is not designed to explain completely all the details of our product (service). If it did, I'd be out of a job. The purpose of our literature is to be a reminder of some of the highlights after one of our representatives has had an opportunity to suggest specific application to our customer's unique situation. May I suggest we arrange a time at your convenience. . . ."Then go on to negotiate for open spots on your calendar. When they insist that you send literature, suggest some salient points in the literature they should be sure to notice. If you know anything about their situation that particularly applies, mention it. Say what you can to cause them to remember that they asked you to send it and to make them eager to read it.

Send a cover letter with the literature with reference to the fact that it was requested. Mention something from your previous conversation that would remind them of it and that would apply to their particular situation. Close with a paragraph suggesting you will be following up soon. Reiterate the benefits of an interview with you. Write notes on the brochures in longhand with a felt-tip pen. On the face of the envelope write, "Personal information you requested."

If they admit to being not interested, come back with, "Obviously you have a good reason for feeling you would not be interested; would you mind sharing it with me?"

Indifference

Indifference is the most common form of resistance you will meet with on a cold call. The most common cause of indifference is that the prospect does not see a need to talk to you any further. Remember that the need must be in the prospect's mind. If it is not there, you must put it there or it will not exist for the prospect at that moment. Another cause of indifference is prejudgment. The prospect prejudges something about you, the company you represent, or the product or service you sell. Indifference, as with most forms of resistance, is easier to prevent than to cure. Many techniques for preventing and responding to indifference are detailed throughout this book. Let's review them:

Prevention

▪ 1. Did you come up with a satisfactory answer to the question, "Why should the prospect listen to me?" When prospects are indifferent, mentally they come to this conclusion: "Based on what I see and hear so far, I don't see enough reason to set aside my planned agenda to spend any time with this salesperson." H. L. Mencken said, "Injustice is relatively easy to bear. What stings is justice." When you have a good reason for prospects to listen to you and they brush you off, they have a problem. When you don't have a good reason, you justly deserve a brush-off. You have a problem.

▪ 2. The words you use are important. Choose them carefully. But how you sound is even more important. Do you sound like a time waster or do you sound like a knowledgeable professional? Do you sound like you are reading or have memorized a script, or do you sound friendly, conversational, real?

▪ 3. Are you putting the emphasis on what it is you are selling? That is going to cost money—a negative reaction in the prospect's mind. The more bells and whistles you talk about up front, the more it's going to cost. Ideas are free— and good ones that relate to the prospect's world are welcome.

Response

▪ 1. "Trouble in River City"—put the emphasis on the need, the problem, the pain.

▪ 2. Ask one of the alternative forms of *why*. You must find out what lies behind the indifferent remark the prospect makes in order to know how to proceed.

▪ 3. Ask an "Are you satisfied with . . ." question. This brings a need out in the open.

▪ 4. Paraphrase the prospect's indifferent remark. Try to make your paraphrase expose the hidden need.

▪ 5. Ask a "just supposing" question.

▪ 6. Tell a story about a customer of yours in a similar situation, who had a problem common to those in that situation. Ask, "Have you ever experienced anything like that?"

▪ 7. Refer to a trade magazine article about a typical problem in the prospect's industry. Again ask the preceding question.

▪ 8. Ask, "Is there anything about your present situation that you are not completely happy with?"

Taking on the Competition

Another form of indifference comes from the prospect who is buying from one of your competitors and everything is satisfactory. Try this series of questions:

> Mr. Prospect, as long as I'm here [or have you on the
> phone], would you mind if I get your answer to a few
> questions?
> What are the things you like most about doing business
> with your present supplier?
> Why are those things important to you?
> What is it you like least?

Sometimes prospects won't tell you what they don't like
about the competitor, but often they will. And when they do,
you have some valuable information. Besides, you didn't have
to put yourself in the position of knocking the competition.
They told you what they didn't like.

You may have some additional questions depending on
what is said in response. Be careful you don't directly knock
the competition. Keep your ears open for any hint of a need,
any possibility that you could do something better in the area
of preference or help them to avoid any dissatisfaction. Then
summarize with something like this:

> Mr. Prospect, just supposing we could provide all the things
> that are important to you and we could help you avoid the
> things you don't like, and we could [add an additional benefit
> or inducement], you would want to know more about it,
> wouldn't you?

You won't get a yes answer to that last question in 100
percent of the cases. But going through this kind of questioning process will get you a lot more business than retreating
from "I'm satisfied with my present supplier." Besides, prospects will know where to find a real pro whenever they need
another source of supply. You gain on your competitors not
by putting them down but by outclassing them.

The Ultimate Neutralizer of Resistance

I can sum up in one word the ultimate neutralizer of
resistance: persistence. No, not high pressure, not being

pushy. There is a difference between discriminating persistence and high pressure. That is, as long as everything you say
in being persistent is for the prospect's reasons, not yours.
When everything relates to the prospect's world, not yours,
it's amazing how persistent you can be without offending.

It's no points in your favor to be labeled pushy. Yet I rarely
ever see sales lost because of too much persistence. But I've
seen many opportunities to make sales lost for lack of it.

Boyan's Best Bid

And now for my all-time favorite appointment clincher.
Over the years this one got me through countless doors that
were almost shut by one of the previous mentioned forms of
resistance. It goes like this:

> Mr. Prospect, I wouldn't begin to tell you that you need what
> I have. That is for you to decide. But I guarantee, you will get
> enough profitable ideas from our interview to make it well
> worth your investment of just thirty minutes. Can we do that
> now, or would tomorrow morning at eight o'clock be better?

If there is any chance of a need, if there is the least spark
of interest, it is difficult for a reasonable person to turn you
away with that offer.

Here is a roundup of ideas that will help you persist when
they resist:

• *Be prepared for resistance*. Don't let it take you by
surprise. In the planning stage, mentally rehearse what you
will do when a prospect gives you any of the various typical
resistances. After a while you won't need to rehearse anymore. Your responses will become second nature.

• *Relax*. When you hear what sounds like it could be
indifference, skepticism, procrastination, smokescreens, or
objections, don't be too quick to answer. Your first response
should be to relax. Hang loose! Cool it! Get in the habit of

taking a deep breath just before you punch those telephone buttons or just before you walk into the prospect's office. Do it as soon as you hear an objection. You will be in a much more relaxed emotional state and better able to respond to the resistance.

- *Listen.* Hear prospects out. Listen with a sincere desire to understand their point of view. Avoid any hint with body language or words that you are eager to step on their lines and start giving your answer or that you imply any judgment to what you hear. You may be champing at the bit to answer, but don't do it. Listen for the feelings behind their words. They will give you the best clues how to proceed.

- *Paraphrase.* When you hear vague generalities or suspect a cover-up of a need, restate the prospect's words in more concrete language. End the paraphrase in the form of a question that seeks agreement to your version of what was meant.

- *Narrow it down.* If the prospect gives you a definite reason why you are not being granted an interview, find out if it's the only one.

- *Question it.* Use a tactful form of asking why. Continue probing for a need.

- *State a benefit that relates to a need.*

- *Suggest a time for an appointment.* Always be thinking in terms of *when* not *whether* the prospect will grant you an interview. Don't hesitate at the conclusion of your benefit statement. Take the initiative to suggest a time. Don't ask the prospect when it would be convenient. You suggest alternative times, the sooner the better.

If despite your best efforts prospects still refuse to grant you an interview, they are not saying no to you as much as they are saying no to themselves.

I hope I haven't given you the impression that the techniques suggested in this book are guaranteed formulas that will get you an appointment with everybody you want to sell. If you have ever heard about the superstar salesperson who can sell anybody anything, don't you believe it! That's more like superstar ego talk.

Baseball players can't expect to bat a thousand. But by practicing the fundamentals, they can increase their batting average. Likewise these techniques won't get you through to everybody you want to reach, but they will increase the percentage of your sales per call. And just like baseball players who have a healthy batting average, you can take your high percentage to the bank.

Whatever you do, don't let the people you can't convince to buy prevent you from selling to the ones you can convince.

Techniques, for the most part, are something we do or say to a prospect. But never lose sight of the things we do or say to ourselves. Those can be far more important. We started out considering the effect of the fear of rejection. If there is call reluctance due to this fear, you will not have a chance to apply the techniques. Getting rid of that fear is something we do or say to ourselves.

Self-image was mentioned several times as the catalyst that makes the techniques work. Self-image, by its very definition, is something we do to ourselves.

But there is one more critical attitude we choose that has an impact on the effectiveness of techniques and that is our intent. I've heard some salespeople say, "When I make a call, I imagine prospects have some of my money in their checking accounts. And I'm going in there to get some of it back!"

If that is your intent, you had better be a good actor or prospects will see the dollar signs in your eyeballs. You will be "smelling from selling," and you'll find yourself quickly on the outside looking in.

Of course, we must use techniques to be effectively persuasive. Skillful execution of techniques is a measure of our professional expertise. And we set goals. After reading Chapter 3, you know I'm a confirmed believer in goal setting. But goals are what we want; prospects could care less about them.

It seems like a contradiction to advocate setting goals on one hand and to concentrate on benefits to the customer on the other. To resolve the contradiction, we have to confine goal setting to the planning stage. When we are in contact with prospects and customers, our goals must be put on the back burner. Because the only way we will satisfy our goals is to satisfy theirs. Remember the story of the young lad who went to see the wise man on the hill to find out the secret of success. As the wise man suggested, we must look out the window to see the people in the marketplace instead of looking in the mirror to see ourselves.

All things considered, the nonverbal aspect of dealing with resistance far outweighs the importance of the words you choose. But remember, it's the attitude you bring into the relationship that forms your nonverbal response. And that attitude is a choice you make.

Many unpredictable things happen in sales relationships. One thing that is absolutely predictable is that you will meet with resistance. It's the very reason for the existence of the sales profession. Be thankful for it. Let its challenge be a part of your professional growth.

Chapter 16

MAKING IT WORK FOR YOU

Adult education is one of the fastest-growing industries in recent years. That sounds like an understatement to those of us in this profession as we see the phenomenal growth.

Billions of dollars are spent every year on a profusion of books and manuals; audio, video, and computer-based programs; seminars; and consultants, all focused on helping people become more effective on their jobs and in living their lives. You could never compute the total investment in these programs, as you would have to factor in the dollars of revenue lost by revenue producers taken off the job to participate in some learning process.

Corporations are the advance guard of innovation in training adults and they pick up the biggest share of the tab. Corporations are also on the cutting edge of designing methods of accountability to ensure that their money is wisely spent. The buzzword in corporate training is performance. Top decision makers found out long ago that training efforts are a total waste unless there is a performance payoff in the real world.

One of the best methods that training-wise corporations use to protect their investment is known as the learning contract. Those who are granted the privilege of adding to their professional growth at the company expense must commit in writing to what they intend to do differently as a result of their training experience.

I suggest you make a learning contract with yourself in order to capitalize on what you learned from this book. If you are in the habit of underlining or otherwise marking the places in a book that were important to you, that's fine. If not, go back over the book and pick out the ideas that could be especially helpful to you. In particular, reread Chapter 3. How will your performance change as a result? Set some new performance goals for yourself. Put them in writing, make them specific and measurable, and date them.

As I mentioned earlier, people resist doing this. Remember my friend who wanted to play the guitar and threw his written goal statement in the wastebasket. Most people are like that when it comes to changing routine. It is easier to fall back into old comfortable habits of doing what produces some results—that earn a living, that get by—so why change?

We resist change for a reason that I believe is an illusion. And that is, it just seems easier to adapt to whatever inconvenience is brought on from settling for less—less personal satisfaction, less financial reward—than it is to adapt to the inconvenience of doing what is necessary to make a better life.

If you would choose to enjoy the rewards of a bigger dimension in life, the joy of a greater use of the potential talents and abilities you have, let me suggest an important thing you must do: YOU MUST FORM NEW HABITS. Because, if you keep conducting your affairs in the same way that you have been habitually in the past, you can only expect to get the same results. If you want to produce better results, then you must do things differently. And this doing must become a habit. If we do not deliberately choose to form productive habits, it is most probable we will unconsciously form habits that are more pleasing but less productive.

Horace Mann gave us this bit of wisdom: "Habit is like a cable. We weave a thread of it every day and at last we cannot break it."

Good luck and good selling.

NOTES

1. Albert Ellis, "Rational Psychotherapy," in *The Journal of General Psychology*, 1958, 59: 35–49. For a fuller discussion, see Albert Ellis and Robert A. Harper, *A New Guide to Rational Living* (North Hollywood, Calif.: Wilshire Book Co., 1975).
2. Maxwell Maltz, *Psycho-Cybernetics* (West Nyack, N.Y.: Parker Publishing Co., 1960).
3. Viktor Frankl, *Man's Search for Meaning* (New York: Simon & Schuster, 1970).
4. Jard DeVille, *Nice Guys Finish First* (New York: William Morrow, 1978).
5. Erich Fromm, *The Art of Loving* (New York: Harper & Row, 1956).
6. See Robert Conklin, *The Dynamics of Successful Attitudes* (Englewood Cliffs, N.J.: Prentice-Hall, 1963), for the details of his philosophy.
7. Lewis Carroll, *Alice in Wonderland*, in Martin Gardner, ed., *The Annotated Alice* (New York: Clarkson N. Potter, 1960), p. 88.
8. *The Music Man* by Meredith Willson, © 1957 Frank Music Corp. and Rinimer Corporation. Song "Ya Got Trouble" © 1958, 1966.

INDEX